When It All Comes Down, It All Comes Down to This...

Live in God's Love

When It All Comes Down It All Comes Down to This...

Live in God's Love

© 2019 by Ken Johnson

Published by Ephraim Enterprises

ISBN 9781793822291

Creative Team: Jan Mathers, Louis Dvorak, Linda Johnson, Gwen McIntosh, Emma Johnson, Missy Kitchell

Unless otherwise indicated, all scripture references are from *The Holy Bible: New International Version.* (1984). Grand Rapids, MI: Zondervan.

Printed in the United States of America

Table of Contents

Chapter One – Nosedives

Everything in my life seemed to be up and to the right until nine years ago, when I found myself in an emotional death spiral.

I got out of the blocks right. I had a good family and a good upbringing. I was naturally entrepreneurial. I started saving money when I was eight years old, pulling my wagon through town, selling my hand-picked wild blackberries door to door. I had my own Christmas tree lots starting at age twelve. I partnered in a tax preparation business with my college Economics professor. I saved every penny I could. I had a goal of having a net worth of a million dollars by the time I was thirty, and at age twenty-nine, I was on course and almost there.

However, eight years after graduating from college, in the middle of financial blessing, I changed course. I began to revise my definition of success.

I walked away from my main source of income, a thriving partnership, leaving eighty percent of my net worth on the table. I went from being a thirty-three percent owner in a multi-million-dollar enterprise to shepherding a small church. I accepted an invitation to care for an interdenominational church congregation of thirty people.

As a twenty-nine-year-old minister I earned a tenth of what I had been making, and was living off of savings, small personal investments and my wife's part-time income as an RN, but that didn't stop me from loving what I was doing. I decided that helping people was more important than making money. Not that the two are mutually exclusive. I just felt I was created to be more of a care-giver than a money maker.

I dabbled in a few passive investments in my spare time, and I had plenty of spare time. I still loved business, and my successful years in the business realm helped me lead well in growing churches.

Our little church of thirty people grew to become a church of three hundred. Then I pastored another church that grew from six-hundred to three thousand.

Be it ministry or business, I got used to my life, and the things in my life, getting better, not worse, getting larger, not smaller, stronger, not weaker, brighter, not darker. That was the trend of my life for fifty-nine and a half years.

That's when I went into an emotional nosedive.

When depression first struck me, I thought, "O.K., this is something dark and new. I'll just do what I've always done, I'll fix myself." It's just that the harder I tried to fix myself, the deeper I fell into the pit of depression.

I felt out of control; full of anxiety and overwhelmed with worry. I couldn't see anything but darkness in my future. My mind ran away from me.

Over a period of six months, my psychological engine stalled, and I went into a downward plummet. I became a helpless, hopeless people-helper. I plunged into what the Christian mystic St. John of the Cross called la *noche oscura*, "the dark night of the soul."

How did it happen? Did I have any warning signals? Actually, my gauges had red-lined but, busy helping others, I ignored the warning signals.

People depended on me, so I hid the problem with a smile and kept going. I spoke to thousands every week, and counseled dozens of others. I tried to disguise my progressive depression, but my family and closest friends saw what was happening.

What in the world is happening to me I asked myself? *How did a happy, energetic people-helper like me become a weary, worried, depressed human being?* I felt that I was in a gravitational death trap that I couldn't escape, no matter how hard I tried.

Most people have experienced minor depression; that's just part of life. When depression deepens to the point of major dysfunction it is called 'clinical depression.' Left untreated, minor depression can lead to deep, clinical depression - a breakdown where a person reaches rock bottom and stops functioning in a normal way. According to the National Institute for Mental Health, "Major depression is one of the most common mental illnesses, affecting 6.7% of American adults each year." [1]

---

[1] Brandie Coskie, *Depression: Facts, Statistics and You* (Healthline Newsletter)

Twenty-six percent of Americans say they have found themselves to be on the verge of an emotional breakdown. According to the Mental Health Foundation, one in five will suffer from clinical depression. These percentages, along with suicide rates, have increased appreciably over the last few decades.

The percentage rises sharply among those who are care-givers – people who spend a large amount of time helping other people. I'll say more about that in a minute.

Depression robs people of the ability to feel pleasure, hamstrings their health and can even be a major factor in suicides. According to The World Health Organization, depression is the leading cause of disability world-wide!

I've briefly defined what deep depression is, but if you or someone close to you is experiencing their own dark night of the soul, I am sure that you want to know why people become depressed and how to pull out of an emotional free-fall.

As I write these words today, I feel like I'm the happiest, most content, most blessed person in the world. I'm enjoying life immensely. I'm this way after being, nine years ago, in a place where I had no hope for my future.

I want to tell you how I came to a place of hopelessness, and how I went from gloomy hopelessness to unprecedented happiness.

Nosedive

Without saying a word, my friend Tom pointed his airplane toward the ground and went into a steep nosedive. Sitting right behind him in his tiny aerobatic plane, I tried to say "no!" but nothing came out.

Just before we plowed into the ground, Tom pulled out of the dive, headed straight up, turned the plane upside down and let out a huge laugh. *It's not funny Tom* I thought to myself! Two years later, alone in his plane, Tom failed to pull out of a nosedive. I lost a good friend. I'm glad I wasn't with him when he crashed.

Not long afterwards, I came close to crashing in a different way. I found myself, a person dedicated to helping others, urgently needing help because I was heading into an emotional nosedive. Here's how it started.

Cowboy prophet

He came up to me after I finished speaking at a Sunday morning service at Westside Church.

"Can I talk with you a minute?" he asked.

"Sure" I said, "Let's stand over here."

When we found a private place, he just stared at me with a fiery gaze. After speaking four times that weekend, I was tired, and my defenses were down, so I was vulnerable to criticism.

The cowboy prophet growled, "God told me to tell you he is going to strike you down. He will deplete your finances, ruin your health, smear your reputation, and expose your wicked heart. Your life is about to come crashing down."

His angry words knocked the wind out of me.

Was he really speaking for God? I wondered. Was my life going to come crashing down? Maybe his disheartening prophecy was already starting to be fulfilled.

Nine years ago, I loaned the lion's share of our retirement funds to two friends who were successful land developers. Because of their good track record (and my foolishness) I didn't ask for any collateral. Long story short, the development company went belly-up and my wife Linda and I lost our entire investment.

On top of that, Westside Church, where I was head pastor, had run out of seating space, and we were adding a 10,000 square foot addition, and I felt great financial pressure because soon after we started building, the United States slipped into recession.

Even worse, I had just found out I had two eye diseases – glaucoma and macular degeneration. Two more tragedies, (which I will talk about later), struck home at the same time. Depression hit me head on at full speed.

While I was trying to rise above all I was facing, the cowboy prophet punched me in the gut emotionally and totally knocked the wind out of me. All I could say in response to his harsh words was, "I hope you're wrong."

"Well, I am not wrong," he answered back. "Just as God judged and cast down wicked King Ahab, so he will destroy you."

Fighting depression, illness and financial loss, I went home, turned off the light in the bedroom and curled up in bed. The slimy octopus of depression wrapped itself around my legs and pulled me under.

Most of us have experienced depression. Ups and downs are part of life, but when *mild* depression becomes *wild* depression, things get crazy.

Care-Givers

Giving care and helping people, vocationally or voluntarily, is a noble calling, but it can be mentally and emotionally taxing.

Social workers, teachers, child-caregivers, health care workers and others who spend their days caring for others might be called "People Who Pay to be Vulnerable."

A friend of mine, a police chaplain, told me recently, "Almost every cop I know is self-medicating with alcohol, pornography, anger, food, or some other means of masking.

They deal with so much junk that it eventually pulls them down."

An online article on this subject says, "Depression can be stealthy, even for the most resilient officer, and can take a physical and mental toll on the mind and body if it goes unrecognized and untreated. Unfortunately, the silence within police culture discourages the acknowledgment of depression ... This silence cannot continue. Every year, just as many officers die by their own hand as do officers killed in the line of duty. Yet, the silence continues." [2]

The same factors that lead to discouragement, depression and suicide among police officers also plague veterans. In 2013, the United States Department of Veterans reported that suicide is the 10th-leading cause of death in the United States, and Veteran suicides, fifty percent more common than non-veteran suicides, is a national concern. A study completed two years ago reported that more than six thousand veterans have been committing suicide every year. That is sixteen precious lives snuffed out every day." [3]

In recent years, more soldiers have died by taking their own lives than have died in battle during that period.

Likewise, many ministers in the United States struggle with discouragement, depression and emotional exhaustion. An article entitled, "What is going on with pastors in America?"

---

[2] Mark Bond, Faculty Member, _Criminal Justice_ at American Military University, _Police Depression: The Silent Killer_(https://inpublicsafety.com/2014/09/police-depression-the-silent-killer/ (Sept. 3, 2014)

[3] "_VA National Suicide Data Report,_" www.mentalhealth.va.gov (Sept 2018)

recounts a recent study of ministers which found that seventy-one percent of pastors are stressed out and burned out. And that affects their marriages. The study found that seventy-five percent of the pastors surveyed felt they did not have a good marriage.

Little did I know, when I became a minister, how much stress people-helpers, including ministers encounter. I thought you just love people and share words of wisdom from the Bible with them a few times a week. How hard could that be?

I did just that with thirty people. But if you love God's word and you love thirty people, next thing you know, you've got sixty people to teach and care for. Then six-hundred, then three-thousand.

People who hear you share from God's wisdom in the Bible and share from your own life, warts and all, want you to be there with them in their best times and worst times. Their baby's birth, their weddings, relocations, major spiritual advances, baptisms, financial dilemmas, loss of jobs, their unemployment, attempts to escape addictions, loss of loved ones, and finally at their funeral.

As a minister, there is just not enough of you to meet all the needs you would like to meet. That is one reason depression rates are so high among ministers.

Another social genre where depression rates are high is parents without partners. Many single parents in the United States face financial, relational, and emotional tidal waves. Losing a spouse and being saddled with sole responsibility for raising good kids must feel like being a Shetland pony with a Sumo wrestler on your back.

According to the National Institutes on Health, people caring for relatives or patients with dementia have a risk for experiencing depression thirty times greater than that of non-caregivers.

People who strive to provide the best possible care for their loved one often sacrifice their own physical, spiritual and emotional needs, setting themselves up for exhaustion and depression.

Help!

I was pretty much a stranger to depression until it snuck up on me. I sure didn't have as much compassion for depressed people back then as I do today.

Even now. it's hard for me to explain how dark and fearful deep depression is. I wavered between having a single thread-like strand of hope and being totally hopeless.

I felt that everything in my life was pathetic. Everything was depressing. Everything that was said to me, and everything that happened to me. Everything was negative. I couldn't read the newspaper or watch the news on TV. Everything, literally everything, seemed like bad news. I couldn't read novels, and if I had read the first chapter of this book, the one you're reading right now, I probably would have thrown it down and walked away.

Can you relate? Have you ever lived at that address? Are you there now? Do you know someone who is fighting depression?

I wrote this book especially for people who help other people, who urgently need a beam of hope in the midst of their dark depression.

Being a teacher, counselor and minister, I had listened to accounts of depression from many people. I tried to really listen and give good advice, but when I experienced depression, I realized how hollow the well-meaning words of a helper can sound to a person caught in the grip of gloom.`

Negative questions haunted me: Will I ever get out of this emotional quicksand? Can I endure any more pressure? Does God really care? Will I be a victim of depression? Am I going to lose my job and let my family down? Will I have a total breakdown? I desperately needed hope.

I knew I was in trouble. But I saw the trouble as something I needed to handle by myself. I was flying through a storm, the worst one I'd ever encountered, but I would just have to keep going until I got through it. One of the greatest hinderances to my healing was that I saw my depression as a sign of weakness.

I worried about what my emotional plunge looked like to the church I led, and to my friends and family. I was hiding everything, trying to tough it out on my own. I was a minister and ministers aren't supposed to need help. My wife, Linda, knew about our financial loss and my health issues, but I kept my emotional battle to myself. In the midst of my storm I was trying to stay calm. Reading gauges. Just trying to keep the plane in the air. That became harder to do as my depression deepened.

My condition worsened because I dealt only with the symptoms of exhaustion and depression, but not the causes.

I waited too long to admit I needed help. I had always been a strong, decisive leader, but I was afraid that if the people I led, including my wife Linda, saw my weakness, they would lose respect for me.

I remember when a lady that I knew from church stopped me on the sidewalk downtown and said, "Pastor Ken, why are you frowning? You're a good man and a good-looking man with a good smile. Lighten up. Smile!" I promptly pasted an artificial smile on my face and tried to make my face tell lies about my heart. Ever been there?

I worked hard at appearing cheerful, thinking that if I changed my thinking it would change my feelings. I wasn't being hypocritical; I was just trying to keep the plane flying until I got better. To people who didn't know me well, I probably seemed positive, but I was becoming more and more negative in my view of myself and my life.

Hollow

As my depression worsened, I tried to shake my blues by doing things I loved to do. I decided to take my bow and arrows and head for the Oregon coast and hopefully be restored in the process of chasing elk in the forests. Hunting recharges my battery, and coastal forests have always been medicine for my soul.

When I got to the coast, the wind was blowing about thirty miles an hour. It's hard to hunt in those conditions, but I headed into the woods anyway. Soon after, I noticed a beautiful, cedar tree with brownish-orange bark, lying on the ground. It had obviously been snapped in two by the wind.

The tree looked totally healthy. The bark looked healthy. The limbs looked healthy. The foliage was a healthy dark green. But the tree trunk was hollow. I don't know if that's normal for cedar trees, or if just this one tree was sick inside. I just know that when I stood by the tree, a little voice inside said, "Like this tree, you look healthy on the outside, but you're not so healthy inside, and to help others effectively, you need to become healthier on the inside." I was fighting a slow-motion implosion.

How are you on the inside? Do you feel hollow and empty? What do your emotional and spiritual gauges, the feelings in the deepest part of you, say?

Maybe you are beyond red line right now. Or maybe you are concerned about someone who is. I pray that what I share in this book will keep you, or keep that person you are concerned about, from becoming a pile of ashes.

As my depression deepened, Linda could see the smoke coming from my engine. My close friends could see it too.

I forced myself to keep going, to stay up later, to get up earlier, to work harder, to learn and earn happiness. One close friend, a physician who was on the church leadership team, pulled me aside and side. "Ken, you've got to learn how to say, every day, 'That's enough.' You need to be accountable to a handful of friends regarding how many hours you are working."

I put together a team comprised of the doctor, my wife, my assistant and two others who knew my life. They held me accountable for working less than fifty-five hours a week. They tried to help me learn how to say, "Enough is enough." I didn't do very well. They had me do a two-week time study and I averaged 74 hours of work a week.

The group tried unselfishly and sincerely to help me. Their concern and support probably helped me postpone my emotional nosedive, but I failed to follow their recommendations fully, and I eventually shut down the group because I gave up on being able to downshift. Until I reached the point of complete desperation six months later, I downplayed the signs of pending crisis.

The needles on my warning gauges were pointing the wrong direction. I felt cold. Even when the sun shone, I felt cold physically and cold in my soul. If life comes in seasons, this was my Arctic winter.

There were demons on my dance floor, inviting me to join them in a dance of hopelessness.

Up to this point in my life, I had seen myself as a strong, positive, independent person. Most of the people that I knew and that I helped perceived me as such. From the solid ground of self-confidence, I had winched a lot of people out of deep mud. I had been successful socially, financially, vocationally and spiritually.

Then I began to experience mild panic attacks. I felt like I was falling. That's not just a metaphor, or an emotional feeling. I literally felt the physical sensations of falling. Like being in an airplane when it hits a big air pocket and drops. Or a carnival ride. When an attack hit, my stomach was in my throat. It was like you feel when you fall off a cliff in a dream.

At the same time, I was on the National Board of our church, making a lot of trips to the church headquarters in Los Angeles. I was the chairman of a committee that was called on to lead the way in an investigation that ended with a popular church president stepping down. The process was ugly, and it fried my wiring.

But a crisis at the church I led taxed me even more.

John (the name has been changed) was a bright, gifted member of our leadership team at Westside Church. He was good with people and he was a talented teacher. I put him in charge of our serving teams, which involved about 1,000 people. I felt that John would probably take my place when I stepped down as lead pastor.

It was reported to me that John was speaking against me, and winning people over to himself, kind of like Absalom did with his father King David. I'm a pretty trusting person, and I just couldn't believe what I was being told.

When John said he wanted to start a church of his own in town, the elders and leaders at Westside asked him to wait one more year; they had seen a couple of cracks in his foundation, character flaws he needed to work on for a year before going out on his own.

John decided not to follow the advice of the elders, and he started a new church in Bend.

The new church grew rapidly. Over an eighteen-month period about five hundred people, one fifth of the Westside congregation I pastored, left us and joined John's church. At Westside Church, the hundreds who left with John were dearly missed. The mass exodus hit me hard emotionally, and it crippled the church financially. I was desperately trying to keep the ship afloat.

I kept quiet about it publicly, but inside it killed me. Every weekend a new family would be gone. "Oh, they're going to the new church, John's church," someone would say. I felt that God wanted me to keep my mouth shut and not speak against John or his church, but I was dying inside.

Dealing with illness, financial loss, building challenges, denominational governance, and a large church split pulled me down. I was diagnosed with PTSD. Every time something happened that made me feel rejected or betrayed, I subconsciously went back to the painful moment when John left and others went with him. I kept reviewing and reliving that soul-scarring event.

Too late?

Thank God, just in the nick of time, I got help from people who understood emotional breakdowns. They helped me pull back on the stick and pull out of my spiral before I crashed. They threw me a rope and pulled me off the face of the cliff, but recovery was slow and painful.

If you or a loved one are experiencing depression or emotional exhaustion, I want to help you in the same way some friends and counselors helped me.

Don't let pride stop you from seeing the severe danger in your situation. You may be a top-notch caregiver, but right now you need some help. You might be a teacher, a counselor, a doctor, a single parent, a nurse, a dentist, a law enforcement officer, a veteran, a coach, a CEO, a parent, a minister, a social worker, or a family caregiver. You might be the spouse or parent of an exhausted people-helper.

It's easy for people who help people for a living to be blinded to their own need for help. We're the helpers, not the helped. We are so used to monitoring other people's emotional gauges that we stop watching our own. Danger signals at this point may be as simple as a funny sound coming from our plane engine, or as advanced as a deadly spiral.

How about it? Do you wish you were someone else? Is it hard to get out of bed and face the day? Do you feel tired all the time? Are you sleeping too much or not enough? Do you feel nothing you do is good enough? Are you easily agitated or angered? Do you see half-full glasses as half empty? Does life seem dark and discouraging? Have you ever thought of checking out?

Your problem may be situational. It may have physiological roots, or it may be the result of some terrible things that happened to you or someone you love. It may be the sum total of all of the above. Regardless of what caused your nosedive, the plane is headed down, and something needs to happen before it's too late.

But please hear me out. It is NOT HOPELESS.

You're not alone.

Your loved one who is in a nosedive is not alone.

Many, many people are secretly struggling with burnout and depression. I know what you're feeling. I know your depression seems inescapable, but it isn't. In the words of the morning." (Psalm 30:5)

After the first stage of my recovery, I began to review my journal entries from my dark night and set out to gather stories and information about depression. Out of that has come this book – my story - which I believe will bring hope and healing to you or your loved one. I'm writing to show you how to survive and thrive. I'm writing to help you go higher than you've ever gone before, and to help you stay there.

You can get through this with help. Your spouse or friend can get through depression with your help. You have a weapon. You can, he can, she can, not only survive, but go on to thrive.

Chapter Two – When It All Came Down

My friend Larry (the name has been changed) is a gifted businessman who always favors others. He's generous and he's there when you need him. He's one of the most positive people I know.

Larry never had a day of depression until the day his wife and infant son were kidnapped by a man who took them into a forest, where he raped and stabbed Larry's wife, Jennifer. After he left, Jennifer crawled to the edge of the road, carrying her son, where she died.

As a man committed to helping others, it was hard for Larry to understand how anyone could be so evil. Depressed, he considered pulling his life tightly around himself, and letting others fight their own battles. But in his brokenness, Larry kept doing kind deeds and helping others. Slowly he rebuilt his life. He eventually remarried, developed a thriving business, and never lost his compassion for wounded people.

Larry's crash wasn't the result of him helping people, but it could have been the end of him helping people. He could have become so shrouded by his depression that he couldn't see the needs of others. He kept holding out a helping hand. Because of this, he bounced back with amazing resilience.

A few years after his wife's death, Larry experienced his second nosedive. His best friend and business partner, Chuck, was killed in an avalanche while they were hunting together in the Shoshone Wilderness area in Wyoming.

Larry and Chuck were about fifty yards apart, walking through waist-deep powdery snow, when they came to the edge of a precipice above a small canyon. As they started down the slope, Chuck yelled "Larry!" just as the snow began to slide on the icy base of a frozen creek. Larry grabbed some nearby branches and held on tight as the snow slid out from under him.

Moments later, Larry called out, "Chuck! Chuck are you OK?" No answer.

Larry ran down the hill and dug frantically in the area where he thought Chuck was, but to no avail. He didn't reach Chuck in time. He had lost his business partner who was his best friend. He made big sacrifices to make sure Chuck's wife was taken care of financially.

Just a few years later, the bottom fell out of Larry's life for the third time. He was heavily leveraged in the real estate market when everything crashed in 2007 and 2008.

Larry went from having an eighty-million-dollar net worth to a negative thirty-million-dollar net worth in a short period. Developed building lots that had been worth $100,000 slid to a market value of $15,000 in just a few months, even though $20,000 worth of infrastructure work had been done on each lot after the ground had been purchased.

With only a few million in reserve, Larry continued to make his payments as he met with the banks and asked them to allow him to pay interest only on his loans until he got his head above water again.

Three of his banks said "yes" to his proposal, but two banks, seeing buzzards circling Larry's developments, called his loans, even though Larry had not missed a payment.

With a small cash reserve and ten different developments financially frozen, Larry laid off most of his one hundred plus employees, many of whom had been with him for almost a decade.

Larry nosedived. He fell sick and found it almost impossible to get out of bed. He had failed others who depended on him. On his worst night, he lay curled up like a baby on the floor of his bedroom closet. I'd never seen Larry have even a hint of pessimism. I was worried for him. I called him several times a week, sharing encouragement. I prayed that he would pull back on the stick and pull out of his nosedive.

I'm not a psychologist or a psychiatrist. I'm just a person who feels it when my friends hurt, and as I talked and prayed with Larry, we were able to discern some of the causes of his extreme collapse. We discerned four factors that seemed to play a part.

Factor #1 was situational. Negative circumstances, beyond Larry's control, were an obvious factor in his nosedive. The 'Great Recession' torpedoed his ship, and all of his assets sank to the bottom.

Factor #2 was spiritual. Larry and I both felt that there was a spiritual element in his emotional dysfunction. The devil, the evil being who Jesus said robs, ruins and kills, was pouring spiritual gasoline on Larry's emotional wild-fire.

Factor # 3 was relational. Larry is kind and compassionate. He told me that having to let go employees who had worked for him and his company faithfully for more than a decade was like being stabbed in the gut. Deep depression often has a social / relational causative factor.

Factor #4 was physical and chemical. Larry had overdrawn his 'adrenaline account.' He was spinning too many plates for too long. He wasn't getting near enough sleep. He was too busy trying to fix things to exercise. The physical toll added to his emotional disorder.

I watched with joy as Larry came back amazingly fast financially, spiritually, socially, and emotionally. He's stated several times since then how much the 'four factors' idea helped him understand his main battle-fronts and wage war on four fronts.

Several years later, when I was in my first-ever steep emotional plunge Larry reminded me of what I'd shared with him about the four factors. He reminded me that negative circumstances were one of the four major causes of my depression.

Not only had I experienced severe financial loss personally, but also loss at Westside Church. The hundreds who left with my assistant and started a new church in town, were dearly missed. The mass exodus hit me hard emotionally, and, as I mentioned, it crippled the church financially. I was desperately trying to keep the ship afloat. Disaster waited in the wings as my depression deepened.

Then something even more devastating happened. Not long after my depressing encounter with the self-proclaimed prophet, my father-in-law, Sheldon, died in a solo plane crash.

Linda came outside where I was working in the yard and said, "Ken, dad just crashed his plane and died." She was in shock, and her words stunned me. Sheldon was a primary leader in my life, a close friend, and my main business partner. Even as I hugged Linda, I felt the gravitational pull of my own emotional nosedive increase.

The cowboy must have been right.

Things happened to me and then within me that I never imagined would happen. As a means of self-preservation, I began to bury my emotions. Day after day I would stuff negative and painful thoughts, then pull myself up by my boot-straps.

Secretly, I was in the darkest of dark times, and I almost wished I'd never been born.

I continued to counsel hurting people, but at the same time I was encouraging and helping them, I felt like I was sinking in quick-sand.

I'm convinced that many people who help people have been in a situation like this. Maybe you're a physician who really cares, and you find yourself facing a baseless lawsuit. Maybe you're a vet who can't escape your nightmares or a teacher who feels like you're all alone. Maybe you're a nurse in a care home and your favorite resident died. Maybe your ship has been robbed by pirates, or you're worn out from endless serving, or maybe you've just cared and cared for others until your care-er broke.

More than once I came to the church platform to speak, looked up and saw the diminished crowd, and asked myself, *"How far will this exodus go? Will everybody leave? Can I even make it through this message, or will I break down up here in front of God and everybody?"*

I felt I had nothing to get out of bed for. I had to hold a mental gun to my forehead every morning to force myself to move.

Emotional graffiti

The walls of my mind had been sprayed with emotional graffiti.

Does God really care?

Why hasn't God helped me?

I won't make it through this.

Something worse is coming.

I'm about to have a full-on nervous breakdown.

I'll lose my job.

I'll be disrespected.

I had always thought of myself as a productive person. I was proud of how I could keep going strong in the face of stiff resistance.

Suddenly I could hardly force myself out of bed in the morning. My energy was diminishing, and my creativity was comatose. Dark clouds of fear concealed my sunlight. I felt bad about being a people-helper, a leader, and yet being so depressed. Everything seemed negative. I wrote in my journal:

> *I feel like I am being driven by something evil*
> *into the pit of depression and despair.*

When Larry experienced emotional exhaustion, I was there for him. I prayed with him, encouraged him, sent him scriptures, and watched him recover emotionally, spiritually and financially. Now that the shoe was on the other foot, Larry was there for me, checking in almost daily.

Another friend who supported me was my close friend Stan, pastor of a church in Montana. Stan had experienced emotional meltdown two years before I did. He spent two weeks at The Center, a counseling facility in Seattle, where he was helped immeasurably.

As he saw my meltdown, he implored me to go to The Center where he had gone for help. Denial, shame and pride held me back until I came to the place where I felt like I was on the edge of a black abyss, and just one little nudge would put me over.

For the first time in twenty-four years, I asked the church for a summer sabbatical. I didn't want to be, or appear to be, a pathetic weakling. I'd always been a strong leader; feeling weak and weary was new for me.

The elders sensed the seriousness of my situation and took it one step further. They asked me to agree to stay off campus and away from the church all summer. They assured me that the thirty people on the church support staff could handle things while I was gone. Feeling like a debtor, I told the elders that I'd come back in September a hundred and ten percent, ready to rock and roll.

Internal bleeding

June was rough. I didn't know how to rest. I'd forgotten how to relax. I watched TV, read novels, slept in and felt worthless. What was I producing? Nothing? What was I worth? Nothing.

July was worse. Some friends offered us their house in Mexico for a two week stay. I thought, surely that will warm and brighten things for me, so we headed south of the border. It was strange, very strange. Even though the outside temperature was ninety degrees a cold grey fog hid my soul from the sun and chilled me to the core. Mentally, I was all alone in an igloo at the North Pole.

I was progressively haunted by thought about the church: *"Are things falling apart without my leadership?"* Or on the other end of the spectrum, *"Will things go so great in my absence that the church leaders will find out they don't need me?"*

I felt that the whole summer was one big waste. I lost interest in my hobbies - fishing, hunting, golfing, hiking and biking. Things that had been fun and exciting became blah. Instead of getting stronger, I grew weaker. For the first time in my life I felt hopeless and helpless. My mental challenge was overwhelming me.

Maybe depression and burnout are only abstract ideas to you. They were to me until I experienced them. Let me just say this: once you experience chronic depression, you will NEVER forget it.

Perhaps you, or someone you care for may be standing on the edge of an emotional cliff, experiencing deep depression for the very first time. Or perhaps you've struggled with emotional exhaustion for an extended period. It must have been miserable for Linda to watch what was happening to me.

In mid-July, six weeks into my sabbatical, I confessed to Linda, "I told the church leaders I would come back full of energy and ready to go. And here it is, the middle of the summer and I'm an emotional rag doll." Unbeknownst to me, she was feeling desperate and had called Stan for insight on how to help me.

When we got home from Mexico, Linda entered my office at home and saw tears running down my cheeks. She implored me to go to The Center. Desperate, and feeling like a failure, I packed up my stuff and headed for Seattle. When I checked in to The Center, I felt like a little boy starting kindergarten; vulnerable, weak, childish, and scared. On top of that, I felt ashamed, fearing that others would think (or find out) I'd gone bonkers.

Are you too proud to get professional help? I was. Are you so used to helping others that you can't even picture asking for help?

I felt like I was sliding down a huge hill toward a cliff and I couldn't stop. I knew the feeling because two years earlier I had done just that.

I took two friends to the steep hills on the Oregon side of the Snake River. We marched an hour straight up a steep hill, chasing chukars, hardy birds that were imported to the US from places like Afghanistan, Pakistan and the Himalayas in Nepal.

We parted company at the top because I wanted to hunt a slope that was too extreme for my friends' tastes. My dog and I started across the slope and headed for some rocky crags I was sure held chukars.

Ten minutes later, I took a step and lost my footing. I began to slide down the hill, forty yards above a hundred-foot drop off. I clawed desperately at the grass and tried to dig my heels in, but the snowy hillside was too steep. I remember thinking, "When will they find my body?" I cried, "Help me

God!" Just five yards from the edge of the cliff, I slid into a rock the size of a traffic cone and stopped abruptly, my heart beating out of my chest.

It took me fifteen minutes to slowly slide my way back up the hill to where I could get my shotgun and stand up.

Now I was sliding down a steep mental hill, and praying for a rope or a rock, or anything that would stop my slide. The rock that stopped me came in the form of the caregivers at The Center, the things they taught me, and the things God showed me. They prevented me from going over the edge of my cliff.

The Center took away my computer and my phone for an entire week. They said it was their policy. I guess they wanted my full attention for a week. *"Next thing they'll do,"* I thought, *"is wrap me in a straight-jacket."*

I was a control freak, totally out of control. In the past, when faced with daunting problems, I just worked harder and longer, and conquered them. Not now. I couldn't control this malady or overcome it by working harder.

Not only was I a control freak totally out of control, but now that I was at a counseling center, I was a control freak under the control of someone else. Could it get any worse?

In my first session with a licensed counselor at The Center, my counselor told me there were some medications that could really help with my depression. I said, "Thank you, but I'm biased against medication, especially medicine for mental or psychological dysfunction." Looking back, I see that I considered myself too spiritual or too manly for mental medicine.

The counselor told me that people with clinical depression usually needed some kind of medication to help simmer their emotions down before they could address their deep, deep sadness. I began to take the medications that I am still taking today, and I am thankful for them!

They placed me in a room with a nice guy named Frank who was struggling with depression and pornography. (Counselors have told me that pornography is often used to mask pain and depression). Frank was a man of faith like me. I had to ask myself, *What kind of faith do Frank and I have to end up in a place like this?*

Every person at The Center had a daily session with their primary counselor along with four or five group sessions geared to helping us overcome our problems.

They gave us a journal and challenged us to record what we were learning. I wrote in my paper journal several times every day and snuck out my iPad at night and wrote a bunch more. As a matter of fact, I wrote down twenty pages of notes regarding what I was discovering, with my counselor's help, about myself and my emotional emergency.

The Center said they would give us the tools we needed to overcome our emotional problems, but we would have to use those tools wisely in the days, months and years ahead. They said journaling would help us deal with what was going on both inside us and around us. As I journaled, I felt like pen and paper captured some redemptive thoughts that had, until then, stayed just out of reach of my consciousness.

At the same time, I felt like I was very close to a total breakdown. Something was fogging my mind. I wondered if it was the depression, or the depression meds I was taking.

I had psychological vertigo. If you're sick in an airplane, they tell you to keep your eyes on the horizon, on something static. My horizon, my static mental foundation, had always been my own ability to produce, to excel. With that gone I had nowhere to mentally fix my eyes.

As we progressed through my week at 'The Center,' I began to see things about me and my condition that I'd never seen before, and they weren't pretty. I entered this in my journal:

> *Who stole your soul Ken? What stole your self-esteem, your sense of adequacy, self-confidence and self-worth? How did you lose who you are? Why are you depressed?*
>
> *Depression leads to even lower self-esteem. Anxiety and depression speak negative things about who you are, which leads to even lower self-esteem. This is a deadly whirlpool, a vicious black hole.*

Undercover

As I passed the midway point of my week at 'The Center', it began to dawn on me that emotional health would require self-awareness. Here's what I wrote in my journal about this:

31

I have a lot of fear inside. Somewhere along the line I disconnected from my emotions. I ignored the feelings of fear and low self-esteem and masked them with accomplishment and busyness.

My favorite counselor at The Center was Ruth. After several meetings, Ruth said, "I sense that you have experienced some major losses and have not grieved those losses adequately." I reflected on that in my journal:

I disconnected from my own emotions. Disconnecting from emotions turns you into a numb zombie or causes emotions to smolder and burst into flames suddenly when least expected. I have learned here that disconnecting from our emotions often leads to depression.

Ruth asked me to write four letters expressing my gut feelings about the four most painful things I had experienced in the previous five years. I wrote a page for each of the four major soul wounds. Writing these descriptions helped me dig up skeletons from deep underground. When Ruth said I needed to grieve my losses, I asked her, "How do I do that?" She answered, "The two main ways to grieve are writing and weeping."

Recognizing and stating for the first time how much four large losses had bruised my soul was a huge part of my emotional and spiritual healing. Pain that I had ignored for so long came to the surface. Admitting my wounds and writing about them in my journal was cathartic.:

> *When John left Westside and all those people went with him, it slashed my soul. People continued to leave for over a year, and that was the salt in my wounds. People that mattered to me, people I had served for years, left Westside without saying a word. Each new exit was a new stab wound to my heart. I felt rejected. I felt like a failure. I've pushed those feelings down for six years. Taking a scalpel to my soul and lancing the wound has made me feel like a thousand pounds of soul-squeezing pressure was released.*

I remember smashing my finger on a fishing trip once. Purple pressure began to develop under my nail. The pressure kept increasing until I could hardly stand it, so I heated a paper clip and used it to burn a hole in my fingernail. Blood shot out of my finger like spray from a squirt gun.

Similarly, when I let myself grieve past losses, it lanced my infected soul, and poison that had been pent up inside of me gushed out.

I took a box of tissues, drove to a park, found a private place in a little grove of trees and read my four loss letters out loud. I wept like I'd never wept before. Thinking about and describing my hurt somehow lanced my soul and let the poison flow out.

Looking back, I think failing to lance that poison of secret grief would have eventually brought me to a place of dysfunction, and maybe even death. Late attention to the symptoms of depression often leads to deeper depression. Unprocessed grief is a deadly venom.

Linda's uncle, Charles, was bitten by a rattlesnake while fishing on the Malheur River in Eastern Oregon. The poison destroyed several of his organs, one by one, and then it took his life. Unvented grief has fangs and venom.

Mid-way through the week at The Center, Linda asked me to consider staying another week. I said, "No way," but she stood her ground and patiently, but persistently, tried to convince me. She reminded me how precious emotional health is and said she was believing for my full recovery.

One week is enough, I thought. I needed to get home and get on with my life. I didn't want to go through any more soul surgery.

My pride had taken a haymaker to the nose. In the first three or four days at The Center we dug up more skeletons than I had uncovered in my life prior to this. It had been grueling, and I realized that staying another week would mean more pain, so I was going home.

Then something happened that changed my mind.

Chapter Three – Crashes

Smoke was pouring from the plane.

A few years ago, my wife and I landed at the Las Vegas airport. We saw a plane beside the runway that was half charcoal black and still smoking. Watching the news that night, we found out that the pilot, in the midst of his takeoff, noticed smoke coming from the plane, and quickly hit the brakes, skidding to a stop at the end of the runway.

In my dark night, I felt like that airplane looked. Charred. Broken. Out of operation.

I still cringe when I think of my sad condition the first day I came to The Center. I was so confused that it was difficult for me to carry on a conversation. Thoughts of taking my own life in a way that looked accidental crept into my mind, but I quickly evicted them.

As I checked in at The Center, I felt certain I was about to crash and burn. I thought I would have to leave my vocation, and probably even give up on my life mission of helping people live better lives.

I pictured people looking at my emotional crash and saying, "What a sad thing. He always said God wants to give people a deeper, fuller life, but look at his life. He tanked."

I remember trying with all my might to create a positive picture in my mind, a picture of me recovering, but I just couldn't bring that picture into focus.

When I came to The Center, I had no hope. After being there a week, I was experiencing a few bright, shooting stars of hope that would pierce the darkness in my soul and then be gone in a few seconds.

On my seventh and final day at The Center, my bags were packed. I said "goodbye" to several patients, most of whom were staying for a second week, which is the norm at The Center. I was attending my final class, the only class we had for men only.

Bill, the class leader, said something that stopped me in my tracks: "Many men think it takes courage to ignore their losses and wounds and go on as if nothing happened. Actually, it takes more courage for men to acknowledge buried wounds and face them honestly. Real men will make themselves vulnerable, even though doing so is very difficult."

He went on to say, "Some people think they are being strong by ignoring, or not admitting, pain. In reality, the strongest people are the ones who feel pain, accept pain, understand pain, and learn from it."

Right then, I changed my mind. I went and signed up for a second week at The Center. My two primary counselors were pleased, and they challenged me to continue to search ruthlessly for the factors that contributed to my crisis.

The counselors began to help me see the real reasons for my brokenness. 'Help' is a key word in fighting depression. As you'll see in the next chapter, I finally learned how to say "Help!" I was aware of the negative situations in my life that played a part in my depression, (things like our huge financial loss), but I needed help to become aware of the inside factors, the psychological, spiritual, social and emotional elements.

It helps to know the causes of your mental midnight. In chronic depression, you feel like you will be in a dark cave for the rest of your life. Clues to how you got where you are can be a tiny beam of light, giving hope that you might make it out after all.

Anti-aircraft

That evening as I sat in my room, my thoughts went back to some of the things Larry had shared with me regarding his three seasons of emotional crisis. He said that in his visionless darkness he felt like a blind man in an unfamiliar room with no doors, desperately searching the walls for a message in braille that would give him the key to escaping.

Every time he had to let another employee go or received another negative phone call or letter from one of his lending institutions, it pulled the rug out from under him again. He started taking depression medications that had some weird and serious side-effects which actually made his depression worse.

He thought his business career was over. Wondering how he could provide for his family, he pictured himself stocking shelves in a grocery store and had to admit to himself that he didn't even feel capable of doing that.

I found comfort in the fact that two men I totally respected, Larry and Stan, had gone through the dark valley of serious depression and had come out the other side. However, in some of my gloomier moments, I thought, *They made it out, but I don't think I will.* Once a vibrant sea of energy, I had become a murky, muddy puddle.

If you are seriously ill, and the medical community is unable to discover the cause of your disabling illness over a long period of time, you languish in your illness, not knowing what it is. What a relief it is when doctors discover the identity of your malady, and help you eradicate the things that cause your illness! In the same way, I began to discover some of the causes for my psychological illness, and to understand some of the actions I could take to help me recover.

The staff at the counseling center helped me reconnect by giving me four specific gauges to monitor my condition. These gauges were related to my depression: Situational factors, emotional causes, physical issues, and spiritual components. I marveled at how these gauges matched up with what God had already shown me when I was supporting Larry years earlier. I wondered if, as I helped Larry God had been gently equipping me for my own up-coming battle before I even needed it.

Causes of crashes

Do mental and emotional crashes have anything in common with airplane crashes?

The most common cause of airplane crashes is *pilot error.* PlaneCrashInfo.com analyzed over 1,000 commercial airline crashes and found that pilot error was a factor in just over half of the crashes.

One thing that pushed me into the pit of depression was an obsession with my own pilot error. While I certainly erred when I made a six-figure loan to a friend without asking for collateral, it did not deserve the degree of blame I assigned it. I see now that self-blame played a large part in bringing about my *emotional depletion.*

We are psycho-somatic beings. Our souls (Greek – psyche) and our bodies (Greek – soma) are interwoven and deeply affect one another. My emotional illness and depletion were exacerbated by my physical depletion.

The counselors at The Center perceived that I was beating myself up with blame, and it was affecting my physical and emotional condition. I was brutal with myself privately. I felt blame for our financial loss, and for my need for help when I should be helping others. I couldn't seem to forgive myself for my stupid mistakes.

According to the National Traffic Safety Board the second most common cause of airplane crashes is making mistakes in dealing with harsh *weather conditions*. Weather conditions, and how they are dealt with, are contributing factors in 23% of all aviation accidents. I equate bad weather with negative situations. Iced wings, storms, heavy winds, fog, and lightning play a part in many plane crashes.

My encounter with depression was like flying into thunderclouds and getting zapped. In hind-sight, it's obvious that the loss of my business partner and mentor, extreme financial setback, and stress from the demands of leadership at the church, all contributed to my emotional collapse. I was too busy looking for a break in the dark clouds to read my internal gauges.

Here is a third similarity between aeronautical and emotional nosedives: According to Boeing, *mechanical failure* can be blamed for about 20% of today's commercial air accidents. Mechanical failures are to an airplane what *physical problems* are to a depressed person.

My psychological collapse involved other physical problems too.

Three years after my emotional nightmare, I was diagnosed with Parkinson's disease. My physicians told me that Parkinson's Disease usually involves depression, and depression often begins before the person is diagnosed with the disease. They felt like my depression, four years prior, was partly a result of the onset of Parkinson's.

As P.D. progresses, synapses in the brain begin to dysfunction, causing steep cognitive decline. The awareness of the inevitability of mental decline is a psychosomatic factor that tends to billow the fire of depression for people with P.D. I have friends with the disease who have socially imploded and began to live like hermits.

Other physical problems came along with PD. My legs and my left arm and hand began to tremble involuntarily. My face changed, taking on a passive or blank look unless I made an intentional effort with my eyes, cheeks and lips to smile and look alive. I have to keep reminding myself to stand up straight because Parkinson's makes my shoulders slouch.

PD causes sleep problems, including restless leg syndrome. You try to go to sleep but your legs keep twitching every thirty seconds or so. Each twitch feels like you touched your leg against an electric fence wire, as a shock fires down your leg.

I was an adrenaline-driven person, working most days until midnight, then getting up early, usually about 5:00 am. More and more work, less and less sleep. My insomnia was also exacerbated by Parkinson's Disease.

Another common sleep-related aspect of Parkinson's disease is something called REM sleep behavior disorder, where you physically do what you're doing in a dream.

Sleep behavior disorder causes one to yell out-loud in his or her sleep as he or she yells in a dream. In other words, your body 'acts out' some dreams, especially those involving conflict or danger. Several times I've had my right arm drawn back to punch a villain, and been awakened by Linda calling out "Ken, Ken!" In one dream I was lying down on the side-rail of an ocean liner, and I rolled off and fell into the ocean, at which time I rolled off my bed and onto the floor.

Whatever the cause, insomnia can wear a person out and play a big part in serious depression or even mental breakdowns.

A friend of mine once said, "Attitude is a choice." I have never forgotten those four words. Parkinson's Disease is medically incurable, but I don't consider myself to be a victim. I tell people who ask about my condition, "I have PD, but PD doesn't have me." I continue to pursue recreation, exercise and hobbies.

My German Shorthair and my German wirehair pointers still accompany me on bird-hunting trips. They're not surprised to see me trip and fall down several times every day when we are hunting. P.D. added fifteen strokes to my golf score, but I keep golfing. (Sometimes it's more like 'flogging.').

I keep doing everything I can, even though what I can do takes twice as long. It might take me five minutes to button my shirt. I used to be a pretty good typist, but now, unless I type very slowly, I make a mistake about every third word. That has made writing this book a lot harder for me. But it hasn't stopped me.

I continue to pray for healing. I have more compassion for people with physical problems. When I offer encouragement, they know that I know what they feel.

Early on, in dealing with my crises, I made things worse by failing, for the first time in my adult life, to have a strong exercise regimen. My passivity in that area boomeranged on me big time. Exercising was one of my major means of letting off steam mentally and physically, and without steady workouts I came to feel like a fully blown-up balloon, about to pop.

I've never liked taking pills or getting shots. I was proud of my physical and mental health until depression body-slammed me, I hadn't called in sick even one day as an adult. I was of the opinion that my body would heal itself if I just took reasonable care of it.

Through my counselors and my physician, I learned that chemical imbalance is often a major factor in depression. I still steer clear of medication as much as possible, but I now see properly prescribed medication as my friend, not my enemy.

Physical problems can contribute to psychological breakdowns, just as mechanical problems cause airplane crashes. The right medication often prevents crashes.

What other cause of airplane crashes can give us clues regarding possible causes of emotional crashes? Picture yourself putting your luggage, some of your clothing, and most of your privacy on a conveyer belt to be scanned. Why? To prevent sabotage!

According to PlaneCrashInfo.com, intentional sabotage has been the primary factor in eight percent of all fatal plane accidents.

I see a parallel. In my dark season, I felt sabotaged by John when he left our church staff, started a church down the street, and gave a sugar-coated invitation to dozens of individuals or couples from Westside: "I feel like God wants you to be a key person in the new church. Come and be a leader at my new church."

I didn't ever speak ill of John because I felt like God wanted me to just keep my mouth shut and leave the outcome up to Him. And more than a year after his moral failure blew up the new church, John came back to town and asked for forgiveness. I forgave him, but that doesn't mean I wasn't deeply wounded by his actions.

Satan is the invisible terrorist who uses people, even people who don't believe he exists, to hurt other people. The scriptures say our real fight is not against flesh and blood, but against the evil one – Satan – and his evil deeds.

The thief comes only to steal and kill and destroy; I have come that they may have life and have it to the full. (Jesus: John 10:10).

When someone blows up an airplane full of people they don't even know, it's got to be Satanic. The evil one loves crashes, be they aeronautical or emotional, because they cause death and destruction, which are part of his self-created job description.

Just as airplane crashes are caused by pilot error, weather conditions, mechanical failures and sabotage, emotional death-plunges may result from emotional exhaustion, negative situations, physical illness and sabotage. Feeling the effects of all four of those factors, I began to lose altitude at an alarming rate of speed.

I wasn't sure which straw it was that broke the camel's back, I just knew the camel's back was broken. My emotional disorder reached a tipping point.

After living in Central Oregon for thirty years, I developed acute allergies. An allergy specialist told me that my immune system avoided allergic reaction to pine pollen, sagebrush and juniper trees for thirty years. Finally, after three decades of exposure to Central Oregon foliage, I reached a tipping point, and my body said, "Too much."

In like manner, emotional allergies can result from physical and spiritual problems, emotional short-circuits, heredity, negative situations and spiritual attack. These factors compound one another until your inner person says, "Too much!"

One of the first things my counselors at The Center helped me realize was that my healing involved understanding what happened *in me* as much or more than what happened *to me*.

Given that, let me mention one other major factor in my nosedive.

Hurry and worry

Wounded, and wanting to recover, I got off my maxed-out treadmill. I slowed down and looked inside myself. No one could do that for me, but the right people helped me.

I came to realize that a lifetime of low-grade worry sickness and hurry sickness played a large part in my emotional collapse. I saw that I had been constantly racing time, and that I had lost the ability to relax and enjoy the present moment. Here are some things that I wrote in my journal as I was becoming aware of my inner illness from tension, fear and worry:

> *This morning as I lay in bed, subconscious thoughts that I didn't want to deal with floated to the top of my mind. I suddenly realized that one reason I don't relax is that I don't like what comes to the surface when I slow down. That is partly why it is so hard for me to simply enjoy the present moment.*

I came to realize that my adrenaline-fueled lifestyle was a subconscious cover-up. I was using full throttle activity to make sure that whatever was deep down inside of me stayed there.

I'm not saying that being ambitious and highly motivated is a bad thing. I think God made me that way, but my accelerator got stuck on full throttle.

I even micro-planned vacations, trying to cram two weeks of travel and activity into one week. I always felt like I was on a belly-board in the surf and paddling as hard as I could to stay ahead of a mountainous tidal wave that was about to crash down on me. I could have written a book called *Fear-Driven Life*. Fear pushed me to go harder and harder, faster and faster.

> *Some of the main fears that have been prevalent in my life are fear of failure, fear of rejection, fear of losing control, and fear of the future.*

I worried constantly. I could have won a gold medal in a Worry Olympics. When I worried, guilt would jump on the worry dog pile. Christians aren't supposed to worry, right?

> *I have worried my way into emotional exhaustion. I have a hard time trusting God one day at a time for that day's protection and provision.*

The words 'abnormal' and 'use' can be combined and contracted into the word 'abuse.' Worry is imagination-abuse. Worrying constantly, I was abusing my imagination, using it in a harmful way.

The bow that is always bent will break. I needed to learn how to unstring the bow. I have heard that bees normally buzz in the key of A, but when they are tired, they buzz in the lower key of E-flat. [4] I was buzzing three octaves below the tired bees.

I was weary. Worry makes you weary. Jesus Christ talked a lot about worry. What He said can be distilled into one word: "Don't!" But I couldn't seem to help it.

The good news was that I was discovering the causes of my illness. It's twice terrible to be ill and not know what the illness is. The bad news was that my emotional collapse had several different causal factors. Realizing and pondering that discovery, I came to think, *Maybe coming to understand the hidden roots of my depression will help me fight my way out."*

And fight I did.

---

[4] Uberfacts, https://twitter.com/uberfacts?lang=en (10.12.13)

Chapter Four – Major Overhaul

The government requires airlines to perform extensive periodic check-ups on passenger planes. People need checkups too.

If you are a people-helper, you help others discern and overcome their personal problems, but what about you? When was your last checkup?

The staff at The Center helped me look inward and probe for the root causes of my meltdown. Discovery started with awareness. I became aware that I was broken, and I needed to change. I came to realize that changing for the better began with changing how I think. Changing how I think could change how I felt, and it could even change who I am.

The Bible tells about the Israelites, recently freed from slavery in Egypt, coming to the boundary of the land God promised to them. At that threshold, God told them He would show them which way to go, since 'they had never been this way before.'

Those six words have double meaning. The first meaning is "You've never traveled this particular route – this way - before." The second meaning is "This new venture is going to change you. You've never yet been the person that you will become if you believe me and step out in faith."

Desperation can lead to positive consequences if you do the right things with it. Becoming who you've never been before is unnerving, but I was ready to become the new me. I was ready to acknowledge my condition and take responsibility for improving that condition.

> *I still can't believe I came to The Center. But I did, and now I'm learning to discover and admit broken places in me.*

When I came to The Center life looked pitch black and hopeless. There was barely a spark of hope in my mind. After a week a few small beams of light pierced the dark clouds, then disappeared. Soon after that glimpse of hope, I would descend back into emotional darkness, wondering *"How can anything good come from this? How can I keep going?"*

Early in my second week at The Center, I experienced one of those short bursts of hope, and I quit worrying about myself long enough to listen to a guy with a broken heart.

There were twenty-five hurting people at The Center when I arrived. After spending nine days together in an environment that encouraged transparency, each of us knew that others there were hurting as bad as, or worse than, ourselves. My heart went out to everyone, but especially to two or three patients who had extremely sad stories.

One morning, the grey skies became bright blue, and the brightness lifted my spirits a bit. One of the guys who had shared part of his dark story was sitting on a bench outside The Center, staring at nothing. I stopped, sat down, and asked him how he was doing. "Not very well," he answered. I shared a few words of encouragement just as a counselor walked by and heard what I was saying. The counselor said, "Ken, you are here to get help, not give help. Keep focused on your condition and how you can improve."

Helping people is second nature to me. It's how the Creator wired me. But I tried to follow the advice of the counselor and look inside myself instead of looking inside others.

My attempts to work on my own healing were made more difficult, however, when the staff moved Frank out of my two-bed room and moved in a gentleman named Alan. Alan was really hurting. He paced back and forth by his bed most of the night. He experienced bizarre anxiety attacks. I offered words of hope and encouragement, but I felt like a tiny trickle-charger, trying to charge a dead battery. Alan scared me. Was I looking at a version of my future self?

Are you a person who finds it much easier and more natural to help others than to ask for help? The thing is, if you don't take care of yourself, you soon won't be able, and maybe won't even be around, to help others. That is why they tell adults on airplanes, "Parents, in an emergency, be sure to put your own oxygen mask on before you put one on your child. If you pass out, you won't be able to help yourself or anyone else."

In the years before my nosedive I was trying to help everyone else put on their oxygen masks before I did. I mortgaged too much leisure time, family time and recreational time – essential rejuvenators – in order to help the ubiquitous line of people waiting for help. I didn't understand then what I understand now: People who are committed to helping others are prime candidates for physical, emotional and spiritual fatigue.

Are you so used to helping others that you can't even imagine asking for help?

It takes compassion to be a caregiver. It takes courage to be honestly, properly introspective. You can't fix what you don't face. Jesus said that He came to help people who would admit they needed healing and help. Have you ever undergone surgery? If so, you signed a consent form before the surgeon operated. The same is true with spiritual or emotional surgery.

I know that it's possible to be too introspective and do endless autopsies on yourself. The old saying is true: Too much analysis leads to paralysis. I also know that God didn't get my full attention and cooperation until I realized and admitted that I needed help.

I've read that in the past, shepherds in the Middle East would sometimes break one leg of a little lamb that was in danger of being mauled by predators because it kept wandering off. After he broke the leg, the shepherd would carry the lamb for a few weeks while it bonded with him and mended. I don't think God caused my meltdown, but I sure know that He used it to stop me in my tracks and carry me for a while.

Deep inside

When I came to Seattle, my thoughts were tangled like a fist full of jumbled fishing line. The skilled helpers at The Center patiently taught me how to open up to myself first, and then to others. It helps to have someone assist you as you untangle your thoughts. I remember one of the counselors saying, "The mind is a dangerous place, don't go there alone."

Looking beneath the surface of myself, I saw things in me I'd never seen before. It was as if I put on a pair of polarized sunglasses.

For twenty years or so, my friend Tom and I fished at East Lake in Central Oregon as soon as the ice came off the lake in May. We fished the steep north shore where some big fish cruise and we took turns spotting. The spotter would put on polarized sunglasses and climb the hill. The glasses enabled the spotter to see fish that the rod-holder, standing at the water's edge, couldn't see.

"A five-pound rainbow is 30 yards to your right and 20 yards out," the spotter would announce. The designated fisherman, lower on the bank, then tried to present the fly to that particular fish. We caught submarine-sized trout (All fishermen exaggerate) by seeing beneath the surface of the lake.

In the same way, with the help of my counselors, I began to see beneath the surface of my life, beneath the glare. I began to realize that there was some unhealthy stuff deep down in me that I needed to bring to the surface and deal with. If I didn't do so, I would be destroyed from the inside out.

Unacknowledged wounds and buried emotions often cause depression. Stuffing emotions is like stacking moist hay. The buried emotions smolder inside of us, and when least expected, burst into flame, making ashes of friendships, marriages, and families. Untended wounds burn holes in our souls.

With help, I began to understand that I was seeing life through the wrong lenses. I was operating under the assumption that my personal worth was proven by my performance and my production. Trouble is, I never seemed to produce enough to convince myself that I was valuable. The harder I tried, the more dissatisfied I became. Wrong thinking left me sinking.

The counselors helped me see that untended wounds deep in my soul had infected my thinking, making everything seem negative. My main counselor told me that a good way to turn a negative (-) into a positive was to draw a vertical line through it (+). Since then, when I discover a negative thought pattern, I confess it to myself and to God, knowing that He's better than I am at bringing positives from negatives. He turned a cruel cross into the greatest positive ever (+).

As the shift in my thinking allowed a quick shaft of sunlight to pierce the angry clouds, I began to rediscover hope. Hope began to grow as I nurtured new mindsets and as an act of will, evicted negative thoughts and welcomed positive ones. New ways of thinking were leading me to new hope. Right thinking was the launch pad to propel me into a higher sphere.

Think Different

My roommate at The Center shared some valuable insight with me on thinking right. Frank said, "As we think, those thoughts make a path in our brains, like an elephant crashing through brush in the jungle. Once an elephant moves through foliage and breaks a trail, it will tend to take that same route over and over. Other thoughts – other elephants – also tend to take the same path.

The same is true with mental trails. Once the thought-path is set, the grooves tend to be cut deeper by future thoughts. If the thought-path is negative, it becomes a negative mindset and grooves become graves." After listening to Frank, I wrote this in my journal:

> *Thought patterns create smashed-down paths in the neurons of your mind like elephants in a jungle. I heard this saying recently: "Neurons that fire together wire together." I've got some negative pathways grooved into my mind.*

But I'm learning that our minds have amazing neuro-plasticity. I must develop some good, positive neuro-highways. I must literally form new pathways through my brain.

Thinking positively is a major component of thinking better. On the sixth day of my stay at The Center, our counselor asked a group of us to create an alphabet of words describing positive qualities about ourselves. My heart began to race. I almost got up and left the room. Emotions affect you physically and I literally felt sick to my stomach. I came within an inch of saying, "Excuse me, I'm not feeling well," and leaving. But just then I felt that I was supposed to stay, so I did.

At that moment I literally couldn't think of even one positive thing about myself. I could think of positive things about other people, but not about me. I started thinking about how and who I 'used to be.' Until I was pulled under by depression, I was ambitious, so I put that down for A.

I struggled through writing the list, and to my surprise, the further into the alphabet I got the better I felt. I could sense the Spirit of God helping me. He reminded me of how good my life had been until the last few months. Here is what I wrote:

I am ...

Ambitious

Believer

Compassionate

Determined

Eager

Faithful

Glad

Happy

Inspirational

Joyful

Kind

Loyal

Macho

Nice

Organized

Positive

Qualified

Responsible

Steady

Trustworthy

Unstoppable

Victorious

Wise

eXellent

Yearning to learn

Zealous

When I finished the list, I was amazed. The process of writing down those positive words about who I had been began to pull me out of my emotional swamp. My self-regard went from a negative eight to positive three in thirty minutes. Forcing myself to think positively when I felt negative taught me something about the power of positive thoughts and positive words. It helped me begin to retrain my brain.

After that I intentionally began to think in a new way. I began to train my brain to ignore negative thought patterns, to stay off the elephant paths. A psychological study found that the average person has sixty-thousand thoughts a day. That's a lot of elephants. Paths wear deep quickly.

Deep depression strangles gratitude. You don't feel like you have anything to be thankful for. Your thoughts about yourself and your situation are negative. When my mental pathway – the grooves in my thinking – led to feeling sorry for myself, I decided to take a new path – think thankfully.

The Bible says: "Do not be anxious about anything, but in everything, by prayer and petition, with thanksgiving, present your requests to God. And the peace of God, which transcends all understanding, will guard your hearts and your minds in Christ Jesus." (Philippians 4:6-7) That's great advice!

> *I can do what Philippians 4:6-7 says to do: Pray about everything, be thankful for something.*

I decided to swim upstream against the flow of my negative thoughts, choosing to be thankful over and over until a groove of thankfulness began to form in my brain.

> *Life has negatives. Life is the way it is, but I am going to make the best of the way it is, starting with this moment. As I choose to be grateful for the positives in my life, I will become a thankful person. I take 23,000 breaths every day, I owe God 23,000 'thank you's.*

It was exhausting work at times, requiring constant vigilance over my thoughts but gradually a groove became visible.

Patient, but not petrified

At the same time, I was learning to be more thankful, I was deciding to be more patient. I knew that beginning to form that new habit would take more than a week or two.

My initial attitude when I entered The Center was, "Let's microwave this thing. Let's get me fixed pronto. Show me what to do and I'll fix myself."

As I agreed to stay a second week, it was dawning on me that my fix would not be quick. That is hard to accept in our microwaved, drive-through world.

> *I have learned that it is unrealistic for me to think I will recover from depression / emotional depletion in a few weeks. A 'quick-fix' mentality for me is self-sabotage. My goal must be progress, not perfection.*

Becoming a positive person requires persistence. On days when I was struggling in emotional quicksand, I would try to free myself by reading something positive I'd written in my journal the day before. In my emotional mire, those positive ideas seemed ridiculous. I would stand in the elephant trail and think, "Did I actually write that? I can't even begin to feel that positive about the future right now." It was a Jekyll and Hyde thing. I had to be patient with myself.

That wasn't easy for me because I have the kind of personality that wants to run toward a staircase and jump ten steps with one leap. It's easy for those of us with slam-dunk mindsets to set our eyes on the prize and see only the prize and ignore the steps between us and the top step, but there is no staircase finish line without the middle steps.

> *If I'm batting .001 and my goal is .350, I need to get to .002 first. I'll have slumps, but I'll keep going. If I keep developing the right*

mental muscles I will become mentally, socially and spiritually fit. Don't give up. Just be persistently patient.

Being patient is not being passive. Passivity leads to petrification. I knew I had to be persistent while being patient. Persistence requires great patience and patience demands persistence. I needed to be patient and persistent, but not petrified.

Several times during my dark night of the soul, I came within inches of just giving up and becoming a permanently broken person. Instead, I dug in my heels, pulled back on the stick, and said over and over, "I will not give in and I will not give up."

I am the only person who can control my depression. My motivation and commitment will determine my success over time.

I am so thankful for the Spirit of God! He is also called the Holy Spirit. Jesus said the invisible Holy Spirit would be with every Christ-follower, and Jesus gave Him the title of 'The Helper.' I couldn't have recovered without the help of the Holy Spirit. He gave me encouragement and comfort and direction.

Maybe you, too, have tried to dig in your heels, but it's not working. The nosedive you're in is so steep you can't find the strength to pull back on the stick. There is a story in the Bible about a man named David that might help you win against gravity.

David was being chased by cruel king Saul. He was emotionally and physically exhausted. He had been hit with one wave of bad news after another. Then one day he and his band of loyal soldiers returned home from a raid to find their houses burned to the ground, their families kidnapped, and belongings stolen. The Bible says that David's men, heretofore loyal, gave serious thought to stoning him.

David found himself friendless at the darkest point of his life. Who came to his rescue? No man. No one but God. The Bible says, "But David found strength in the Lord his God." (1 Samuel 30:6) He didn't strengthen himself within himself. He didn't strengthen himself through his circle of friends. He strengthened himself in the Lord.

That's what I did. I had run out of zip. I felt lonely and worthless, but when the Lord was all I had, I found the Lord was all I needed, just like David did.

I prayed for persistence, and God helped me to hold on for life. *I'll come through this thing, and become a better person, or I'll die trying.* But I needed more than resolve, I needed to be refilled with God's Spirit so that His power inside me would become stronger than the pressure around me.

I'm picturing you reading this book. Believe me, I understand how dark things might seem to you right now. I understand you feel that hearing one more negative thought will push you over the edge, but please don't stop reading. Take the next step, even if that step only advances you a few inches. Here are a few possible next steps:

Admit you need help.

As much as possible, sleep.

Try to confide in someone trustworthy.

Let your family and friends help you.

Start talking back to negative thoughts.

Try natural supplements.

Get professional help.

Exercise daily.

Pray.

Keep reading this book.

You're going to see how God brought me through this into victory. Read the next chapter, and then the next. New trails can be blazed. It gets brighter. It might be just what you need. You may not feel like it but do it anyway. Stick with it, even if it hurts.

How does one climb a mountain? One step at a time. You and I don't need enough faith, right now, to finish the journey, we just need enough faith to take the next step. My next step was an important one.

Chapter Five – Lift

Before his death in an airplane crash, my father-in-law, Sheldon, engaged in a lucrative hobby; buying and selling airplanes. We owned a cabin in Alaska, and one time when we stayed at the cabin, scouring ads, Sheldon found a plane for sale nearby that interested him. He asked me to go with him to check out the plane. On the way there, I kept asking about the plane and he kept saying, "You'll see when we get there."

I could hardly believe what I saw when we got to where the plane was. It was a tiny plane that was little more than sticks covered with canvas. "Will that thing actually fly," I asked. "You and I are about to find out," he said with a chuckle.

"There's not enough room for two people in there," I complained. Sheldon sat down in the seat and told me to sit behind him. I had about twelve inches for my body, and I put one leg on each side of him. We were crammed in the funky plane like sardines in a can. Off we went with nothing to navigate by but a hand-held GPS. I said a silent prayer of thanks when we landed.

On the way back to the cabin I asked Sheldon about aerodynamics, how airplanes fly. He had been a flight instructor in World War II, and thus knew a lot about airplanes.

Sheldon explained Bernoulli's principle to me. Bernoulli's principle deals with the relationship between air pressure and air speed. With a typical plane, the upper surfaces of the wings are more curved than the lower surfaces are. The curved upper surfaces divert the air away from the wings and cause the air above the wings to flow faster than the air below. The faster-moving air above the wings has less pressure than the slower moving air below the wings, and the greater pressure below the wings pushes up on the wings and lifts the plane.

A plane with insufficient forward speed has insufficient pressure differential and insufficient lift, which leads to crashes.

Houses need lift too. Just as airplanes need wind beneath their wings, houses need solid and level foundations for lift.

I once watched a house lose its lift, its subliminal foundation. The house was a nice A-frame on the banks of the Sandy River east of Portland, Oregon. Every time I traveled to Portland, I made it a point to notice the condition of the house. Over a period of about ten years the bank caved off until a third of the house actually hung out over the river. Not long after that, the house crashed down into the river.

While observing the results of the final collapse of that house into the river, I thought, during my soul's dark night, *"I wonder if what happened to that A-frame will happen to me?"*

I see a relationship between an airplane crashing because of insufficient lift and a house crashing down because of insufficient foundation. Both of those collapses can be seen as picturing emotional collapse.

Reliable lift

Jesus Christ spoke of the tendency for lives with unstable, inadequate foundations to collapse under the influence of floods, hurricanes, land-slides, etc.

I'll never forget the day Roy, at The Center, a councillor who I felt had genuine concern for me, challenged me about the mental, psychological and spiritual foundation of my life. He began by recounting a story Jesus told about two men who each built a house. One built his house on a sandy, shifty foundation and the other built on a solid rock foundation. When floods came, the house on the solid foundation stood strong, and the other house collapsed and washed away.

Here is what Jesus said in the scripture Roy referred to: "Anyone who listens to my teaching and follows it is wise, like a person who builds a house on solid rock. Though the rain comes in torrents and the floodwaters rise and the winds beat against that house, it won't collapse because it is built on bedrock. But anyone who hears my teaching and doesn't obey it is foolish, like a person who builds a house on sand. When the rains and floods come and the winds beat against that house, it will collapse with a mighty crash." [5]

"The foundation you need," Roy said, "is God's amazing, scandalous love. God paid a huge price to lay down a foundation of love that you can base your life on. You have to learn to trust His heart, even when you can't trace His hand."

Then Roy pointed out to me the most quoted verse in the Bible:

"For God so loved the world that he gave his one and only Son, that whoever believes in him shall not perish but have eternal life." (John 3:16)

I had been familiar with the Bible all my life, but until Roy showed it to me, I had never seen the relationship between the house built upon God's rock-solid word and God's undeserved love for me. I saw myself as one of the 'so loved' people mentioned in John 3:16.

People, just like airplanes and buildings, need foundational lift. Seeing that I was sinking emotionally, Roy challenged me to "build my life" on the truth of what God's word says about His incredible love. The Spirit of God challenged me, through Roy, to build my world-view, my personal appraisal, indeed my entire life, on God's indestructible, unconditional, reliable love.

A new foundation

---

[5] Tyndale House Publishers. (2013). *Holy Bible: New Living Translation* (Mt 7:24–27). Carol Stream, IL: Tyndale House Publishers.

I once heard 'The Prof,' the late Howard Hendricks, a successful educator and businessman, say, "You can't build a skyscraper on a chicken coop foundation." As I progressively learned to base my thoughts on the conviction that God loves me for who I am, I had a solid foundation for my life.

I knew first-hand how important foundations are. Soon after we were married, Linda and I purchased a rental house as an investment. We hired a carpenter to help us touch up the inside of the house, and he became frustrated because the house didn't 'square up.' He said, "Ken, trying to fix the inside of this house is a waste of time at this point. Before we do that, you need to have someone jack up the house, remove the broken-down lava-rock foundation, and put in a nice, new cement foundation." I followed his advice and had a new foundation put in. Our solid foundation cost us 25% of the total cost of house and land.

What I learned regarding building reconstruction, I found to be true with emotional reconstruction also: A good, stable foundation is expensive, but without it, restoration is short-lived.

People in Louisiana know that. New Orleans is sinking. Unlike most of North America, which is built on bedrock, the southern coast of Louisiana is built on Mississippi River silt, which is finer than sand.

Five thousand square kilometers of Louisiana's coastline have sloughed off into the sea in the past one hundred years. That's an area almost as large as the state of Delaware. In some cities, the land has sunk over a foot and a half in the last twenty years.

As the situation worsens, some have resorted to 'mud-jacking' in an attempt to save their homes. Mud-jacking is the process of forcing cement, under pressure, beneath sinking foundations. Even with mud-jacking, many of the homes in Louisiana continue to sink.

In stark contrast to the sagging, sinking Louisiana foundations is the foundation of the *Pentominium*. The *Pentominium* is a dazzling 1,800-foot high luxury tower in Dubai. This tower stands tall and straight because it is based on 20 piles that were driven a record distance, 213 feet, into the earth to reach bedrock. Getting down to solid ground cost a fortune and took immense effort, but there is nothing chicken-coup-ish about the *Pentominium*, and there is nothing chicken-coup-ish about the life God intends for those who believe in His love.

With outside insight, I came to see that I had been trying to mud-jack my soul, not with concrete, but accomplishment. I wrote books and articles, spoke to crowds, developed leaders, and helped people. I loved what I was doing, but I discovered that my reasons for doing what I did were not all altruistic. I'm not saying my motives were all wrong, but they weren't as pure as I thought they were.

I was praying one day, and I asked the Lord if my motives were pure. This thought entered my mind, and I felt like it was sent from Him, "Your motives are pretty good, but not pure. You occasionally bow down to four idols."

I was shocked!

He continued, "The four idols are fear of failure, the desire to be admired, the sin of self-sufficiency, and the need to succeed."

With that, I came to realize there was water in my gas, engine-stopping impurities in my motives. Since that time, I have been able to recognize (with the help of the Spirit of God), when I begin to bow to one of those idols. Those four idols are made up of four lies about what makes me valuable. Together, they say my value and self-worth is based on my performance and production.

Have you ever bowed to any lying idols; idols who said your worth is not measured by God's love for you, but by your acceptable performance and production?

I quit trying to base my worth and self-esteem on my own actions and accomplishments. I began to base my life on God's unconditional, unearned love for me. I began to read the Bible through new lenses. I highlighted the verses in my Bible where Jesus said that God loved us first, while we turned our backs to Him. The distilled message of the Bible is not "God is ticked," but rather "God is love."

I believed that theologically, and gladly shared it with others, but in spite of my belief, I had been basing my self-worth on myself and my accomplishments, not on God's love.

I'm not saying that my production-based self-esteem was the only factor contributing to my depression. I had worn myself out with too little sleep and too much adrenalin-driven activity. I was in the early stages of Parkinson's Disease, which often begins with depression. Negative situations surrounded me like a pack of wolves. I'd been wounded deeply by the exodus of some dear church friends. Many factors played a part in my dark night, but the primary factor was an inadequate foundation. In aviation terms, I lacked lift. In the words of an old hymn: "Love lifted me."

To keep from crashing, I needed counseling, medication, insight, and encouragement. I needed to learn to say "no." I needed to stop being a people-pleaser, and I needed to do my best to bounce back financially. I needed to be with people who loved me. I needed perseverance and endurance.

I needed all of those things, but the first thing I needed was the revelation that I must build all of those things on a "God loves me" foundation. No more mud-jacking.

iTrust

"In God we trust." That proclamation is found on every piece of American currency. It seems to me that the more currency we have, the more currency has us, and the less trust in God we have.

My new basis for living higher and larger started with trust. As Brennan Manning said, "Self-acceptance becomes possible only through the radical trust of Jesus' acceptance of me as I am." [6] Just as I am.

---

[6] Brenan Manning and John Blasé, *All is Grace* (David C. Cook, 2011), 161.

I began to notice what the Bible said about God's love and learn to rest and live in that love. I remember pouring my heart out to God midway through my two weeks at The Center. "Lord, I'm so very tired of being worried and anxious."

Let me say right here that I had a lot of voices in my head at that time. Out of a cacophony of negative thoughts, one voice rose above all of the others, not in pitch or volume, but in sweetness.

"What do you want?" I heard Him ask.

"I want to enjoy life and be able to relax without feeling guilty."

"Then learn to trust me and believe that I truly love you. If you trust in my love for you, I will teach you how to relax and enjoy life."

That was a defining moment for me. It changed the direction of my life. I'll always remember that conversation because it was crucial to my recovery. I drilled down to that bedrock by replacing old thoughts with new, true thoughts.

Thinking differently is called "repenting." I thought differently about God and His love for me, which led me to think different thoughts about me.

I repented. When I say "repent," your probably think of someone in sackcloth, or someone on a crowded sidewalk in a big city, holding a sandwich board the says "Repent."

Actually, the Bible word for 'repent' means to change your mind, heart, self, and your way of life. I repented of wrong thinking. I was thinking wrong things about myself and about God. I decided to believe actually and wholeheartedly what the Bible says in John 3:16. That one verse is the distilled essence of the entire Bible. John 3:16 was a major overhaul for my engine, a new and solid foundation for my life.

With help from the Bible and other books about God's love, I began to arrest fake truth, popular but untrue thoughts about God and about myself. My commitment to thinking right was bolstered by statements in the Bible, like the one in 2 Corinthians 10:5, about taking captive untrue thoughts: "We demolish arguments and every pretension that sets itself up against the knowledge of God, and we take captive every thought to make it obedient to Christ.

Sometimes when I was alone, I would actually speak out loud and say, "That thought is not true," or, "This thought is true." I stopped giving untrue thoughts access to my mental pathways. By intentionally and repeatedly thinking about and trusting in God's love, I began to convert worry and anxiety into enjoyment and relaxation.

Trusting God and His love, rather than trusting in myself to earn favor via production, was not easy. I needed help. I read books by Christian authors that spoke of God's love.

I read the Bible with 'Does-God-really-love me?' glasses on. I found and saved scriptures that spoke about trusting in God and especially about trusting in His love. Here is one of those scriptures: "Trust in the Lord with all your heart and lean not on your own understanding; in all your ways acknowledge him, and he will make your paths straight." (Proverbs 3:5-6)

I memorized those verses and some other buoyant verses that I will share with you later. I repeated the verses in my morning quiet time, and several times more each day in an attempt to develop new neural pathways. I moved toward trusting in God and His love with all my heart.

I soaked my mind and my soul in God's word. Memorizing and repeating these scriptures has been a big part of learning how to live in God's love. Slowly, the detergent of God's love began to lift off the wrong thinking that was caked on my soul.

What could you soak your mind in to help remove the negative thoughts, attitudes and self-images that have stuck to your thinking? Please don't soak your mind in a pool of self-pity, or in alcohol, or drugs, or a bathtub full of bitterness. Soak your mind in positive books, positive scriptures, and positive statements. Don't give up if it takes a long time for the negative grime to come off.

Even though I filled my mind with scripture, trusting God and resting in His love was an on/off thing for me. Some days were better than others. Journaling helped me remember what I learned. I still had a lot to learn, but these positive scriptures and statements slowly began to change me from the inside out and bring me to the place where my life was found in His love.

My feelings go up and down. My faith even goes up and down. But I have decided that I

will trust in you. Even when fear hammers at
my faith, I will trust in your love.

My initial attempts at standing up and moving ahead were awkward, but also adventurous.

Have you ever seen a newborn colt try to stand for the first time? It's clumsy, super-shaky. I felt like that as I began to walk out of my dark night. I would trip and fall, but I got right back up. My modest improvements didn't feel so temporary as they had before. My hope of recovery was beginning to increase.

I remember thinking the day before I packed to go home, *Wouldn't it be something if this whole episode worked out in a way that actually made me a better person, more stable, healthier, and more alive?* I stopped to mull that thought over, and it led to another realization. *That was a positive thought; I actually thought an unscripted, spontaneous, positive thought. It's been a long time since that happened.* I was changing. I had a long way to go, but I was and beginning to see some light. I began to see something else too; something that God sees through the top lens of His bifocals.

True me

All my life I have tried to become a more likable me. There is nothing wrong with that, but the 'accepted by you' me is not usually the 'true' me.

Letting go of my grief, being honest about my soul wounds, and resting in God's love, pulled me toward the authentic me. Basing my life on God's love involved seeing myself as God sees me. Once I learned to see my true self, I began to be my true self.

I had always looked to my performance and production to get my bearings. I was the guy who finally made the A Team. I was the guy who was successful in business. I was the pastor of a large, thriving church. Or was I? Hadn't I just idiotically lost most of our retirement money? Hadn't the church stopped growing? Wasn't I in a desperate mental and emotional state?

> *I've never been this way before, and that scares me and disorients me. My primary point of reference has been my success and productiveness. Is God allowing this season of financial setback and loss of productivity? Is He using it to help me establish a new reference point – His love for me?*

I'm learning to see myself as God sees me. I became convinced that God looks at me with bifocals. Through the bottom lens, He sees who I am now, warts and all. Through the top lens He sees who I was created to be, my full potential. How do I become the person who He sees I can be? It's simple, but it's not easy.

According to the Bible the 'true me' is the person that I am in Christ – the one God loves. I set my heart to be the person

God wanted me to be, nothing more, nothing less, nothing else.

John Newton, who authored the God-honoring song "Amazing Grace," spoke of his personal transformation like this: "I am not what I ought to be, I am not what I want to be, I am not what I hope to be in another world; but still I am not what I once used to be, and by the grace of God I am what I am."

Philosopher and author Soren Kierkegaard spoke of personal transformation quintessentially when he said, "And now, with God's help, I shall become myself."

The book of Exodus in the Bible tells a story about a group of people who spent 40 years wandering in a sandy wilderness asking God to "fix this," while God waited 40 years for the next generation to pray "Fix me." I was done saying, "Fix her." "Fix him." "Fix that." "Fix this." My new request was "Lord, please fix me. Change me."

With help from God and others I changed my attitude, and that changed my life.

When France had fallen to the Nazis, the British outlook was bleak. What Prime Minister Winston Churchill said back then is still true today: "Attitude is a little thing that makes a big difference." Attitude is a choice. There is an instrument on airplanes called an attitude indicator (AI). An attitude indicator informs the pilot whether the plane is flying level, going higher, or going down.

Reading my own AI, I realized that attitude repair was a must. I put myself in the airport shop to repair my engine before I crashed. I will always view this crisis period as my year of major overhaul.

More and more, I'm learning to see myself as living in front of God, and not in front of people. I still value people's acceptance and approval, but it is more important for me to please God than to please people. I am no longer addicted to human approval.

The powerful, invisible Spirit of God, who Jesus said was like the wind, was the God-given wind beneath my wings. He lifted me, but I didn't stay up.

Chapter Six – Down

I remember digging for clams with my dad, mom and brother on the Oregon Coast. Mom suddenly began sinking in the muddy wet sand. She got stuck up to her knees, and we all had to help pull her out. If there is no bedrock, one just keeps sinking, or stays stuck. That truth makes me think of a tragic story I heard the last time I was in Big Lake, Alaska, visiting my son.

Back in the late 1980's, Wasilla paramedics got an emergency call regarding a young lady who had been dip-netting at the mouth of Fish Creek when she got stuck in the mud. Paramedics hustled to get to her before the tide came in.

This was because nearby, just a week before, eighteen-year-old Adeana Dickinson had found herself in a similar predicament. Adeana, who lived in Nevada, was on her honeymoon with her husband Jay. Early one July morning, Adeana and Jay drove a four-wheel all-terrain vehicle down a trail near Ingram Creek to mine for gold.

When their ATV got stuck in the mud, Adeana got off to push, and doing so, buried herself waist deep in the mud. For two hours, Jay tried frantically to pull her out, but the harder they worked, the deeper she sank. Finally, he ran to call 911.

Rescue workers came and fought against the mud and the rising 38-degree water, but they were unsuccessful. Numb with hypothermia, they couldn't quite pull her loose. Six hours later, they retrieved Adeana's body. [7]

Rescuers who came to help the lady stuck in quicksand-like mud at Fish Creek were able to celebrate a happier ending to their story.

Her rescuers said they were energized by knowledge of the fact that in the past 30 years, at least three people had drowned in that area after sinking into the ooze of glacial silt.

Together, they pulled their potential victim out before the rapidly rising tide took her life, and the tears that followed were tears of joy, not sorrow.

My rescue

Depression was a paradox for me. Up to the time of my breakdown, if I got in a jam, I prayed and fought my way out. Now, for the first time in my life, the harder I fought the deeper I sank.

I can't thank God enough for pulling me from my gooey grave of depression. He sent His rescuers – his scripture, some dear friends, medication, His Spirit, His love – to rescue me, and I'll be forever thankful.

[7]Accidents Heighten Rescue Teams' awareness Of Tide's Deadly Force - By Marilee Enge, ADN 8/1/88; Anchorage Daily News (AK) July 16, 1988; Section: National, Edition: Final, Page: A1

Part of my rescue involved revisiting my past. I came to realize that if I wanted to recover, I'd have to uncover. Specifically, I would need to mentally and emotionally revisit my childhood and meditate on some painful memories.

Some people are more vulnerable to depression than others. Genetics play a large part, but all of us have areas of emotional vulnerability. Many of us avoid our area of susceptibility, refusing to acknowledge it.

Instead, we hide our inner brokenness and cover our wounds with fake happiness. In his book, "A Glorious Dark", A.J. Swoboda says that because of this rampant masking "we've become the most numbed culture in the history of the world. We take pills. We watch movies. We're alcoholics. We're addicted to food." [8] Swoboda quotes Brene Brown: "We're the most addicted, medicated, overweight, drunk culture ever. Why? Because we're masking real, deep pain and brokenness." [9]

One of the things I covered my soul wounds with was busyness. There are no rearview mirrors on jet planes. Having finally slowed down enough to reflect and look back, I also finally perceived my history of approval addiction. One of the largest social bruises on my soul had been buried inside of me since I was in junior high school. That's when my addiction started, as I describe in the next session.

---

[8]A.J. Swoboda. *A Glorious Dark*, (Baker Books, 2014), 62.

[9]Brene Brown, *Daring Greatly: How the Courage to Be vulnerable Transforms the Way We Live, Love, Parent, and Lead.* (New York: Gotham, 2012)

Are you tired of struggling against depression's strong suction? Are you weary of trying to renovate your life, only to have your efforts thwarted?

Now, eight years after my crisis, I realize that part of my calling in life is to help rescue people who are caught in the deadly suction of deep depression. That's why I'm writing this book.

Don't give up, friend. You can yet be rescued. You can be a more thankful, generous, compassionate people helper than you were before. You can make it through this, and you can help others even better than if you hadn't had your nosedive. As Carl Jung said, "Knowing your darkness is the best method for dealing with the darkness of other people." [10] I came to realize that my restoration would be a lot like the renovation of that rental house I bought. I needed to fix the roof, repair the walls, and level the floors, after I rebuilt the foundation.

Likewise, I needed to fix my emotional exhaustion, my adrenaline addiction, and my fear of rejection after I replaced the old foundation, – my production and accomplishments – with a new foundation – God's unstoppable love for me.

God invested His strength into my weakness. He deposited His soundness into my brokenness. When I was unable to be strong in myself, I learned how to become strong in Him. Letting go of my pride and admitting my brokenness was the first step to receiving His healing.

---

[10] Carl Jung, *Letters – Volume 1*, July 31, 2018

My hunting dog, Chasity, broke her leg. I took her to the vet, and he put some pins in the bone and told me that when the break mended, it would never break there again. The location where her bone was broken would become super-strong after it healed.

Maybe something similar happens when God heals a person's broken soul.

One of the main areas my soul was wounded, one of the things that caused depression to hit me so hard, was an unhealthy desire, an unrecognized desire, for approval.

B Team

In junior high I decided I wanted to be popular. It seemed to me that being a Christian would make me unpopular at school. I set my sights on being a successful athlete instead. Heart-first, head next, I drifted away from God, my family and my childhood faith, and I shifted from wanting God's approval to focusing on man's approval.

I wanted so badly to be an athlete. I was on the B Team in Junior High basketball. We played in the oldest gyms, with only a handful of fans. Our jerseys were old and worn. I had number 13, and the 1 was coming unstitched. I felt like my jersey had a big L on it, for Loser. We B-Teamers called ourselves 'the scrubs,' trying to cover low self-esteem with humor.

Not having much natural athletic ability, I had to work extra hard to even make the B Team. I became a gym rat. Any time I heard of an open gym, I went. I dribbled a basketball up and down the streets at night under the streetlights. My headway toward becoming an athlete was slow.

Then my dream came true. One of the players on the 8th grade A Team sprained his ankle and Coach Williams called me up to the top eight for the most important game of the year. I was in heaven. I didn't think I'd get in the game, but just to be part of the team and to wear one of the eight new A Team uniforms was enough.

Then the bubble burst. The morning of the big game dawned. I jumped out of bed, energized by anticipation. As I walked down the hallway at my Junior High School, Coach Williams came out of his class and caught up with me.

"Hey Ken, how are you?"

"Great coach."

"I'm afraid I have some bad news, Ken." (Long silence)

"Mike's ankle healed faster than we thought it would, and I'm going to let him take his place back. Sorry, Ken, but you're back on the B Team.".

Blinking away tears, I just kept walking. Perhaps that is when fear of rejection became such a large, negative factor in my life. I had a fear that people would think me to be boring, unattractive, incompetent and unworthy of their approval.

85

I didn't realize in the years after my athletic demotion how badly it had scarred my soul. Seems silly, doesn't it? I mean, I lived in America, I had two great parents, God had blessed me in so many ways. But what happened to me when I was wet cement in the seventh grade put ugly footprints in the concrete of my soul.

In spite of the footprints, I refused to give up and when to college on a partial athletic scholarship.

Fear of man

There is an interesting term that shows up over and over in the Bible: 'Fear of man.' Often this fear is contrasted in the scripture with the term 'fear of God.' The word 'fear' in these two phrases doesn't usually mean 'being frightened of a person, or of God, because they can hurt you.' Rather 'fear' means being aware that you're being watched and being afraid that you will displease the one who is watching you. In that sense, fearing man is living to please people and fearing God is living to please God. In my case, fear of man had a lot to do with my depression.

One day as I was pleading with God to help me slow down and enjoy life, I heard this question in my mind: "Would you worry about not getting everything done if you were the only person on the planet?" Assuming it was the Lord, I thought for a minute and then said, "No."

"Why not?"

"I guess it is because if I was the only one on the planet, and if I failed, no one would see it." That short conversation gave me a startling glimpse of my fear of looking bad in the eyes of people.

Years ago, Andree Seu penned these insightful words about fear of man: "The trouble with fear of man, of course, is that you have a thousand masters instead of one to please. You think fear of God is bad? It's nothing compared to the alternative. Fear of man is a cruel tyranny. It's exhausting, it's complicated, and you're not nimble enough to pull it off." [11]

Desperate to survive and thrive, with help from God and people, I developed the backbone to look deep inside myself. I saw myself when my memory reached back to the eighth grade, with a new clarity. I realized that although I did love the game of basketball, I was after more than accomplishment. I was after acceptance. My childhood desire to please God had been replaced with a desire to impress and please people.

> It is extremely important to me to be liked by nearly everyone in my life. I am learning that I have a 'try-to-please' disease. The need to be liked has fueled my compulsive workaholic lifestyle.

I just couldn't accomplish enough to convince myself that I mattered. I was dad to three amazing kids. I've been faithful to Linda, I kept myself in good physical condition. I ran the

---

[11] Andree Seu, *Fear of man – From Ahithophel to Herod to Dick Morris– Panic at PBS?* Posted Aug. 14, 1999.

Boston Marathon when I was forty-five. I succeeded in business before I became a pastor. I wrote books. I pastored thousands of people. I led the largest church in Central and Eastern Oregon. I succeeded in making good passive investments. I was on our denomination's International Board of Directors. Excelling, however, didn't satisfy me. My high level of achievement just meant that I fell further when I fell.

Another closet skeleton that I uncovered during my depression was production-based self-worth. As I learned more about what led to my emotional nosedive, I found that basing my self-worth on what I produced was the biggest factor in my steep emotional plunge. I was obsessed with proving I was valuable, and I mattered.

Thus, when the self-proclaimed cowboy prophet prophesied disastrous failure over me, the first thing I thought was *I hope he is wrong. He sounds like Coach Williams sending me back to the B-Team.*

So, whether the bearer of bad news was the cowboy or the coach, my response was to be manly, to buck it up and work harder at being impressive and more productive.

The good news is that I am now aware of my impure motivation - the water in my gasoline. I have been able to recognize and refute those four idols, which represent four lies about what makes me valuable. The lies they whispered to me for most of my life is, "Your value and self-worth is based on your performance and production."

He loves me

When I realized what it was doing to me, I slowly began to turn my back on my long-term habit of equating my worth with my work. I started to focus on God's grace (undeserved favor) other than my output. I also set out to learn more about God's amazing love for me. Before I could base my life on God's love I had to know more about that love, so I did a study on love in the Bible.

There are four Greek words for love used in Jesus' day. *Eros* represents erotic love, *phileo* means brotherly love, *storgae* pictures fondness, and the fourth, *agape*, is stronger and deeper than the other three.

Agape is unconditional, totally independent of the recipient's response. It is undeserved and fierce and eternally persistent. Jesus loves with that kind of love. On the cross, He asked Father God to forgive those who crucified Him. Jesus is God's love wrapped in skin.

One of the major accents of the gospels is Jesus' attraction to people who were not very attractive. He ate, talked, laughed and walked with obvious sinners. The Bible says He died for us "while we were still sinners," not after we cleaned up our act. God loves us because He freely chooses to do so.

Agape love is sourced in the nature of the lover, not the merit of the loved one. The Bible says God loves me because of who He is, not because of who I am.

The idea that God loves me without reserve, fully and freely, regardless of my performance and production, is what I call an 'upstream idea,' an idea that goes against my natural way of thinking.

You can 'row, row your boat' gently down the stream of thought prevalent in our culture. A current that says, "No one loves someone who is unlovely or unlovable. If you want me to love you, love me first..."

Have you ever tried to swim against an ocean undertow or a strong river current? You have to swim faster than the current to make it upstream. Likewise, resting in God's love is challenging. Here are a few power strokes that helped me get upstream.

First, I would read the Bible and then take long walks to talk with God. I didn't just talk, I listened. That is, I tried to listen. In my time of deep depression, my mind was tortured by a cacophony of thoughts, loud and negative. When I read the Bible with God-loves-me glasses on, negative thoughts were shoved aside for a few moments. As I walked and listened, I had to use some mental and spiritual discipline, stiff-arming those negative thoughts and leaving space for God's voice.

Think right. Every time you begin to walk on a mental pathway that leads you to depression, replace the negative thoughts with positive thoughts. It's not enough to try to 'not think' negative thoughts. You must go a step further by literally replacing those thoughts with positive thoughts. Here are some positive statements I memorized:

"I will come through this and will be stronger, more compassionate, and more relational."

"Today I choose to focus on hope, optimism and joy. I choose to view life as fulfilling."

"God created me. God loves and values me."

I challenge you to memorize those positive statements and add them to your anti-depression arsenal. If you're not good at memorizing, write a few of the statements on an index card and get the card out several times each day, or tape it to your mirror.

Once you stiff-arm negative thoughts and think right, the next step is to *speak right*. Words have the ability to build you up or tear you down. When you speak out loud, your ears hear your words.

When a giant wave of depression hits you, fight back with words of truth. Speak the truth about God's love for you. If there are others near you, just whisper truth loud enough so that your ears can hear it. If you need to step outside for a minute, do so and speak out loud. Speak out the positive statements I listed above, or these positive scriptures.

"Though you have made me see troubles, many and bitter, you will restore my life again." (Psalm 71:20)

"When I am afraid, I will trust in you." (Psalm 56:3)

"Be joyful in hope." (Romans 12:12)

"May the Lord lead your hearts into a full understanding and expression of the love of God." (2 Thess. 3:5)

Try it for a week. See for yourself how intentionally replacing wrong thoughts and wrong words with right thoughts and words can literally change your life. Don't let down your guard, because negative thinking will leave you sinking.

He loves me not

Not only does the idea of unstoppable, unconditional love run counter to prevalent thinking, it is diametrically opposed by the evil one and his army of fallen angels.

Satan wants us to disbelieve his existence, so he can deceive us without our recognizing what he's doing. He is Anti-Love because he is Anti-God, and as the Bible says, "God is love." (1 John 4:8)

A.W. Tozer was spot on when he said, "The most important thing about a person is what they think about when they think about God."

Satan's primary strategy since the Garden of Eden has been to implant in our minds the idea that God is colonial. That is, God uses us to accomplish what He wants done. "You'd be better off," said Satan to Adam and Eve, "if you acted as your own god. You wouldn't rip yourself off like He is ripping you off now."

Satan works tirelessly to make us doubt. If the devil can't make us doubt God's existence, he will work to undermine our faith in God's love.

Over and over, the evil one will tell us we fall short of what it takes to be loved by God. He paints a false picture of God as some cranky old accountant, keeping careful record of our sins. That's a lie. The truth is, as the Bible says, "Mostly what God does is love you." [12] Unlike our natural resources, God's love is a supernatural resource that will never run out.

What pulled me out of my pit of depression was learning to accept God's acceptance of me. Before I could base my life on God's love, I had to accept His love. I had to accept the fact that God actually, truly, unconditionally, deeply loves me.

Maybe I should write a book called 'The Love-Driven Life' before Rick Warren does. [13]

Maybe, just maybe that 'L' on my forehead meant 'Loved,' not 'Loser.'

---

[12] Peterson, E. H. (2005). _The Message: the Bible in contemporary language_ (Eph 5:2). Colorado Springs, CO: NavPress.

[13] _Purpose Driven Life_ by Rick Warren has sold 20 million and holds the all-time U.S. record for sales of a hardcover non-fiction book.

Chapter Seven – Fuel

"Hey, we're out of gas!"

My friend Mark was sleeping in the passenger seat while I drove his truck to Idaho. As the pickup stuttered Mark croaked "Switch tanks." He showed me where the switch was, and pressing it, I felt a fresh surge of energy.

Frank, my first roommate at The Center, hit the nail on the head when he said, "Switch tanks."

"Ken, here is my perspective on your life, based on what I see and what you've shared with me. You're like a truck with two gas tanks. One tank is filled with people's appreciation of you and respect for you. The other tank is filled with God's love for you.

You're accustomed to running on the first tank, but it has run dry. You need to switch to the other tank and learn more about how to be fueled by God's unconditional love."

Frank's analogy made sense to me. How about you? If you're dealing with depression or burnout, or discouragement or doubt, maybe part of the reason is that you haven't learned how to rest in God's love.

I hope it becomes plain to you, as it did to me, that we were manufactured to be motivated by God's totally undeserved affection. The scriptures say, "God first loved us." His love for me is what fuels my love-based actions toward Him and toward others.

The idea of God loving me regardless of my thoughts and deeds was hard for me to fathom. How could a holy, perfect God love me, flawed as I was?

Maybe you're like I was. Maybe you haven't learned yet how to accept the truth that God accepts you just as you are. Evangelist Billy Graham always invited people at his crusades to step out and come forward as the choir sang a song that begins with the words "Just as I am." It's not "God will love me if I do this or become like this," but rather "God loves me just as I am."

My first fuel tank, my 'I matter because people think I matter' tank was bone dry. I had taught myself to be fueled by earning people's appreciation rather than simply receiving God's free love.

I lost my sense of self-worth and my self-confidence. I lost the ability to think clearly. I lost most of our retirement money and I thought there was a good chance that I might lose my job at the end of the summer.

My friend Don Stewart wrote a book about how to win our spiritual battles and not be POWs. Don, who has counseled countless people, says in his book *Caught Between Heaven and Hell*, "I began to realize that these people's thoughts about themselves, about others, about God, were rooted in difficult, hurting and sometimes, very painful experiences in their lives. ... As a result, ... they believed things like 'God could never love me' ... 'I have to keep proving myself' ... 'All love is conditional.'" [14]

I'm going to marinate my mind and my heart in God's undeserved love every day for the rest of my life. The fact that I have intrinsic value because God values me was beginning to soak into my soul. I wasn't out of the woods yet. I still had a lot to learn about God's ability to bring good things out of bad things.

... but God

Let me introduce you to two amazing pivotal words: *'but God.'* These remarkable words played an important part in my full recovery.

The term 'but God' shows up ten times in the Bible book of Genesis alone. For example, a man named Jacob used these two words when he declared the reason he was not going to give up in spite of tough times. "*But God* saw the fix I was in ..." [15]

One of Jacob's sons, Joseph, learned the same lesson his father learned. After a thirteen-year nightmare of injustice, Joseph saw God's purpose in his trials, and told his betrayers, "Don't be afraid. Do I act for God? Don't you see, you planned

---

[14] Don Stewart, *Caught Between Heaven and Hell* (Deep River Books), 46.

[15] Peterson, E. H. (2005). *The Message: the Bible in contemporary language* (Ge 31:42). Colorado Springs, CO: NavPress.

evil against me, *but God* used those same plans for my good, as you see all around you right now—life for many people." [16]

If you read the Bible, you know that it is not a fairy tale. It's a real book about the real God who loves real people in a real world. Think about this for a minute. The life-giving message of the entire Bible pivots on those two words, *'but God.'*

"... *but God* meant it for good." (Genesis 50:20)

"...*but God* will redeem my soul." (Psalm 49:15)

"...*but God* is the strength of my heart." (Psalm 73:28)

"...*but God* has the last word." (Proverbs 16:1)

"...*but God* directs your actions." (Proverbs 16:9)

So what present situation could you begin to improve by adding the words 'but God?' Might it be, "I'm very discouraged, but God...?" Or, "I was betrayed, but God ..." Perhaps it's, "I have no money, but God ..." or, "My wife abandoned me, but God..." Remember, nothing is impossible with God.

On the Jewish day of Pentecost, a man name Peter stood before a large crowd in Jerusalem and said, "This man was handed over to you by God's set purpose and foreknowledge; and you, with the help of wicked men, put him to death by nailing him to the cross. ⍰ *But God* raised him from the dead, freeing him from the agony of death, because it was

---

[16] Peterson, E. H. (2005). *The Message: the Bible in contemporary language* (Ge 50:19–20). Colorado Springs, CO: NavPress.

impossible for death to keep its hold on him." (Acts 22:23-24)

Note the word "impossible" in that passage. The disciples were discouraged and depressed when Jesus was arrested and crucified. Their Lord was dead, and their future looked bleak. Overcoming what they faced seemed impossible, *but God* ...

The resurrection of Jesus was the ultimate 'but God,' and it still spawns new, almost unbelievable 'but God's.' At my lowest point I didn't think I would ever recover, but God loved me to recovery.

I had to do my part. I got honest about my hidden wounds. I read books about God's love, and memorized statements and scriptures about God's love. And I chose to believe that God was *God enough* and *good enough* to love me just as He loved His Son.

As my two weeks of getting counsel came to an end, I was getting better at disciplining my thinking. I began to recognize when I was on one of those old elephant trails in the jungle. I learned to make a citizen's arrest of those familiar, negative thoughts that led to my nosedive, because they were thoughts that were out of line with God's revelation of His love.

When my imagination would throw a depressing thought at me, I'd attach a 'but God" phrase to the end of that sentence and create a new mental trail. More and more, I learned to think the thoughts that I knew were true according to God's word.

Down to this

When it all came down for me, I could feel the g-force of my nosedive, *but God* actually trumped the evil one, who wanted to destroy me. The upward God-force was stronger than the downward pull of spiritual and mental gravity. Instead of being destroyed, my life would be enhanced.

And that is the message of this book: **"When it all comes down, it all comes down to this: God loves you with an incredible, totally unearned love."**

So, in a way, when I recovered from depression, I was raised from the dead and given a fresh start. God's *agape* love powered my restoration. I see clearly now that Jesus came from heaven to reveal God's love by the words He spoke, the way He lived, and the death He died. Jesus didn't make a habit of pointing His fingers. He made a habit of opening His arms.

God's love is a lavish love. God loves productive people and He loves unproductive people. God loves people who have made a habit of doing good and people who seldom do good. God loves us because He is God, He is good, He is love.

'If love

Most human love is what I call 'if' love. You will love me if I am loveable. You will love me if I return your love. God's love is not an 'if' love. He doesn't love me if I'm obedient, or if I'm dependable, or if I'm popular, or if I deserve to be loved. I had grown up thinking God loves me *if* ...This thought pattern was so ingrained in my mind I was scarcely aware of it.

The Spirit of God, through the counselors in Seattle, pulled me out of the mire. As I prepared to go home, I thought about the inner revolution I had experienced the last fourteen days. Before I came to The Center, I was shrouded with depression. I had lost my appetite and twenty pounds in the months prior to my time at The Center.

And then, two weeks later, as I headed home, I was determined to keep getting better, with God's help.

I packed up my gear, said "goodbye" to my counselors, and headed home from the counseling center. I had definitely begun to build a new life: A life based on the firm foundation of God's agape love. I was a like a bird with a broken wing. I was mending, but I still had a long way to go.

> *Lord, thank you for being so patient with me.*
> *I have a long way to go, but I am seeing more*
> *clearly what it looks like for me to live a love-*
> *based life.*

Yes, I was beginning to live A LOVE-BASED LIFE. My self-esteem, my sense of personal worth, indeed my very life, what I do and why I do what I do, is all based on God's amazing, unearned love for me.

On the six-hour drive home, I thought about the challenges that lay ahead of me. Would my family look at me differently after my weeks at The Center? How about the church leaders? I was sure many people in the church had wondered why I was gone all summer. Some of them probably heard about me going away for counsel. What would they think? I still had ups and downs every day.

On the positive side, I had learned that God's love is not an 'if' love, but an 'I love you *even if* love. I started looking at my own quirks and failures that I thought might block me from God's love.

Your even if's will be different from mine, but everyone has some. One by one, I examined my shortcomings, and asked myself the question, "Can God love me *even if*?"

And I had a closet full of *even-if's*.

Chapter Eight – Even If

When I went home from The Center I had pulled out of my nosedive, but I was still flying just above treetop level. I had promised myself that I would continue my new habit of reviewing what I had learned in Seattle. I continued to review my notes from The Center, memorize and quote positive statements, and learn more about God's love for me.

When I walked through the front door of our home, I received hearty hugs from my wife and my kids. I thought, *"They love me even if I don't deserve it. They love me no matter what."*

A few days after I got home, I met with the Council - the elders of the church. They hadn't seen me for three months and they were eager to find out how I was. I confessed to them that I had barely avoided a full out mental crash. "To be honest," I said, "I'm not at a 100% productivity level, but more like 50%."

I thought they might recommend that I step down as Senior Pastor, but they didn't. "We love you," they said, "And we will take you back right where you are, and we'll do everything we can to help you keep improving". Once again, I encountered unearned, unmerited *agape* love.

Their warm reception made me think of the story about the little boy who was afraid of the dark. His dad heard him crying in his bedroom and went in to comfort him. "What wrong Stevie?"

"I'm afraid Dad. Please lay down and stay in my room tonight."

"You'll be fine without me, young man. Jesus is here in the dark with you."

After a few moments of silence, Stevie tearfully said, "Yes, daddy, but I need Jesus *with skin*."

My wife, my kids, the leadership team at the church – they were 'Jesus with skin' to me. They were a tangible representation of a 'no matter what' love.

A higher grade

Like never before, I appreciated and prized *agape* love, *even if* love. I now think of *agape* as a higher grade of fuel for living.

We were made to run on a higher grade of love. God's love – *agape* love – is a million grades above 'if' love that I spoke of in the last chapter. God loves me even if I am unlovely. God loves me even if I don't love Him. God loves me even if I ignore Him or hurt Him. God loves me even if I don't deserve it. God loves me even if I disappoint Him. God loves me even if I don't believe He does.

God created us because He is Love, and He created us to be filled with and fueled by His *agape* love. *'I will be loved if'* fuel, may motivate us for a while, but will eventually ruin our engines.

Linda and my kids loved me with an 'even if' love. The leaders at the church who welcomed me back, broken wing and all, loved me even if I didn't deserve it.

Home from the counseling center and entering gingerly into day-to-day duties, I began to discover more things about God's startling love, and more things about how His love trumped unlovely things in me.

His 'even if' love

... even if I worry too much.

Maybe you're a worrier. Maybe you know one. Perhaps you've even come to the place I was, where I worried about everything, and therefore enjoyed nothing.

The bad thing about worry is that it strangles your soul and causes you to miss God's message about it: "The seed that fell among the thorns represents those who hear God's word, but all too quickly the message is crowded out by the worries of this life and the lure of wealth, so no fruit is produced." [17] Jesus explained that in this parable the thorn bushes

---

[17] Tyndale House Publishers. (2013). *Holy Bible: New Living Translation* (Mt 13:22). Carol Stream, IL: Tyndale House Publisher

represented worrying, and the seeds in this parable represent "the message." What is "the message?"

God's message is "I love you." The message of God's love is choked out by the thorn-bushes of worry. "For God so loved the world" gets smothered in our worry-choked lives. For too many years, I was caught up in worry. I discovered the best antidote for this was to trust in God and His love for me.

> *God is showing me that I'm past due for learning to trust more. Trusting is the antidote to worry and anxiety.*

"God loves me." Believing that and saying it helps me slow down, quit worrying and live in the present.

> *I must start now to live in the now. I must begin to milk enjoyment from the current moment – to savor the present. Learning to live in the now, being free from regret (past) and fear (future) takes time.*

God loves you even if you're a world-class worrier, but He loves you too much to leave you that way.

... even if I am a workaholic.

Diesel powered vehicles aren't meant to run on gas. When we filled our rental van in New Zealand with diesel, thinking the fuel was gasoline, the van was ok for about ten miles, but then it stuttered and died. It was a costly lesson.

The same is true with what fuels people. Unfit fuel, unhealthy energizers may propel you for a season, but eventually they ruin the engine. You can be driven by love, or you can be driven by fear. You choose.

More than once, I've been called a driven person. I could see that becoming the new me, the true me, the more relaxed and relational me, would be a major change. It would require courage, time and determination.

> *I must treat my workaholic lifestyle as intentionally and seriously as a recovering alcoholic. I must include margins in my schedule and learn how to enjoy relaxing.*
>
> *I must elevate 'being in the moment' over 'doing tasks.' Life smothers without margins. Relationships suffocate in a life without margins.*

As I mentioned earlier, since my mid-twenties I have been attempting to slow down and enjoy life more. Although my accountability team tried to help me with this, most of the gains I made were short-lived. However, after my emotional dive, l learned that work and relaxation are not enemies. In fact, each is essential to the other and time must be made for both in order to operate at your full potential.

Today, I'm no longer seeing success through the narrow lenses of a workaholic.

God loves you even if you are a workaholic, but He loves you too much to leave you that way.

... even if I tend to be a people pleaser.

When I was a little tot, we used to sing a song in Sunday School that said, "There's a Father up above, and He's looking down in love." How much better off we would be if we were as aware of God watching us as we are of others watching us.

The Bible tells us the Lord renounced the religious leaders of his day. He scanned their motives, and the scan was ugly: "Everything they do is done for men to see:" (Matthew 23:5)

> *I often do too much for other people or even let myself be used, so I won't be rejected.*

> *Fear of rejection has been a brutal taskmaster in my life. I'm tired of being bullied by fear of rejection. Fear has painted ugly graffiti all over my picture of the future.*

As I mentioned earlier, I was addicted to people's approval. I lived in fear of being disrespected or rejected. Living my life to please others instead of living it to please God was one of the roots of my constant anxiety. Understanding this helped me build a new life from the foundation up. More and more I can agree with the Bible when it says, "Cheerfully pleasing God is the main thing, and that's what we aim to do,

---

[18] Peterson, E. H. (2005). *The Message: the Bible in contemporary language* (2 Co 5:9). Colorado Springs, CO: NavPress

regardless of our conditions." [18] Who is your audience of significance? Who are you trying to please?

God loves you even if you're a people pleaser, but He loves you too much to leave you that way.

... even if I am a control freak.

I admit I've been suffering from obsessive/compulsive disorder. OCD is based on a desire to control. I tend to want to fix, arrange, organize, tame and control every area of life.

> I must learn to work and rest. I must learn balance. I must learn to TRUST in Christ and rest in His love and acceptance. As I stop trying to control and fix everything, perhaps I will learn to experience and enjoy things. I will learn how to live in the moment instead of living in the past or the future.

I knew that my obsession with control played a part in my emotional nosedive, but I wondered how much I should change. Did God want me to go all the way to the other end of the spectrum and not plan or prepare at all... just shoot from the hip at everything? Was I supposed to be a disorganized person?

> My counselor Shelley pointed out the fact that I am a very organized person. God made me that way, and I will probably always be that way. Resting in God's love will not cause me to

become disorganized, but resting in love will affect my motivation for organization; the 'why' of what I do. That is the transformational thing that is happening in me. What I do is changing some, and why I do what I do is changing a lot.

One day when I was obsessing over something like a pit bull who's locked his jaws on a pant-leg, Linda said, "You know, you can go down stairs and get a drink, sit a few minutes, and then go back up to your office and work for an hour or so."

When Linda said that, a light bulb turned on in my head. I will never forget that sentence. Balance is priceless to a man who seems to have only neutral and overdrive. In four-speed jargon, I had blown first, second and third gear.

My tendency to try to control things is a sign, as I see it, of weak faith. When I'm not sure that God will carry me through and protect me, I protect myself as an insurance policy. Can you relate?

God loves you even if you think you can earn His love, and He loves you too much to leave you that way.

... even if I am sinning.

The Bible says, "All have sinned," so all of us are sinners. Here's another crucial 'but God' found in the Bible: "But God demonstrates his own love for us in this: While we were still sinners, Christ died for us." (Romans 5:8)

So many people see God as a divine killjoy, trying to make sure we don't have any fun. Others see Him as an intolerant parent who consistently points out what we do wrong.

God is not mad *at you*; He's mad *about you*. He is waiting for you to accept the fact that you are accepted and loved in and through His Son.

You don't have to clean up your life in order to be loved by God. He sent His Son to make a way for you to be forgiven of every sin you have ever committed.

God loves you even if you are sinning, but He loves you too much to leave you tangled in sin.

... even if I have deep soul wounds.

Our first response to cuts and bruises in our souls is to cover up the wound in order to diminish pain and avoid negative exposure. I practiced covering up when I went into my emotional nosedive. I'd never experienced depression before, and my instinct was to suck it up and buck it up.

I didn't want anyone to know that I was struggling. As Brennan Manning says, "The imposter – the master disguiser – avoids any significant exposure. [19]

> *When I removed my workaholic bandages, I stopped masking my many negative emotions, including fear. I don't need to be threatened by*

---

[19] Brennan Manning, *Abba's Child* (NavPress, 2002), 56.

that. The surfacing of these emotions is part of my healing process.

God loves you even if you are severely wounded inside, but He loves you too much to leave you that way.

... even if I base my value on my production.

Production-based self-regard was the foundation I had to tear out and replace. As I learned how God thinks about me, and as I learned to think about myself from His point of view, I was able to chisel, pound, and jackhammer slowly until that faulty foundation - personal achievement and the approval of others - was removed.

Feeling better often starts with thinking better. They taught me at The Center that I get to choose how I feel about myself.

God loves you even if your personal evaluation is based on the wrong foundation, but He loves you too much to leave you on that faulty foundation.

... even if I am ill

Two years after my time at The Center, I began to experience tremors in the left side of my body. My facial expression grew somewhat blank. My daughter Kara, who does medical records for neurologists, became concerned and Linda talked me into seeing one of the neurologists where Kara works. He diagnosed me with Parkinson's disease, and that diagnosis was confirmed by the Movement Center at Oregon Health Sciences University in Portland.

My physicians surmised that mild symptoms had begun five years prior, about the time I had my attack of depression. They told me that depression is often an initial symptom of Parkinson's, and that there are no medications or treatments that stop the progression of Parkinson's Disease.

What hit me hardest with the diagnosis was not the physical aspects of PD, but the mental. Parkinson's patients have six times the normal risk of dementia. [20] Some studies indicate that up to 80 percent of Parkinson's patients will eventually lose the ability to think and reason. [21] In spite of that dark prognosis, I didn't fall into depression or entertain suicidal thoughts. My solid new foundation, God's undeserved, extravagant love, kept me from pessimism.

It kept my mind fixed on the truth of God rather than the truth of my circumstances. Because of this solid new foundation, I stood unshaken amidst the storm of PD.

In the same way, I find that my compassion quotient has increased. I'm more sensitive to people who are hurting, more willing to help. Once again, God is bringing good out of bad. I have decided I will stay positive and just face this thing one day at a time. I'm refusing to think l am a victim, because I am a victor who is dearly loved by God.

---

[20] Doidge, *The Brain's Way of Healing,* 38.

[21] Jon Palfreman, *Brain Storms* (Scientific American/ Farrar, Straus and Giroux, New York),

Maybe you are in ill health also. Maybe you are experiencing anxiety attacks, or PTSD, or depression directly in relation to your physical condition. Maybe it runs in your family. It's easy for us to think, *If God loves me, why am I ill?*

The Bible says that as He hung on the cross, Jesus took on all of our infirmities. He was ill, extremely ill, for us. Did that mean the Father didn't love Him? Not at all. And even though I'm asking God to heal me, I am fully convinced that He loves me whether He heals me now, or when I stand before Him in the life to come.

God loves you even if you're ill, and He loves you too much to leave you that way.

... even if _____ doesn't.

Whose name would you put in that blank? You might say, "my father" or "my mother." You might say "my ex." Someone who is reading this will put "my son" or "my daughter" in that sentence.

Regardless of the name or title you would put in that blank, I understand that pain behind it, that it slices your heart. We all want to be loved. The Creator wired us that way.

Who 'less than loved' you? Did that send you into a tailspin? I speak "Grace" over your life right this moment. I want to be a messenger of love and declare to you that I was where you are, but God saved my life. He can save yours.

I've never seen that cowboy prophet again since the day he prophesied my demise. He couldn't have made that prophecy to me at a worse time. I slid down a slippery slope of depression and just about went over the cliff. But God's love saved me.

It appears the cowboy made a mistake in his prophetic zeal. He failed to account for God's love.

God is totally dependable, and His love is as firm as the Rock of Gibraltar. Basing your worth on human love, even the love of Christ-followers, is building on sand. Only God's love is rock solid.

God loves you, even if _____ didn't / doesn't.

... even if I find it hard to trust in His love.

Trust is more than an emotion. It's a choice. If we choose to trust Him, God will prove to us that He is worthy of our trust.

This book is a challenge to you. The challenge is to learn to trust God and trust His love more than ever before. As scripture says, "It is through faith that a righteous person has life." [22] Use the trust you have, and God will give you more because He loves you.

God loves you even if you are finding it hard to trust in His love, but He loves you too much to let remain in doubt.

---

[22] Tyndale House Publishers. (2013). *Holy Bible: New Living Translation* (Ga 3:11). Carol Stream, IL: Tyndale House Publishers.

... even if I don't feel worthy.

Depressed people don't feel worthy, they feel worthless. It's interesting that in my depression, I felt positive about others, but negative about myself.

Here is a statement that stuck in my soul like Velcro recently: "Sadly, many people, even many sincere believers, seem to struggle with their identity, laboring under a sense of low self-worth. Many appear to be thrashing their way through life, striving to prove to themselves and others that they are indeed somebody. What a tragic and unnecessary exercise in futility." [23]

I believe addiction is a form of illness, not worthlessness, and I've discovered that many addicts struggle with depression and/or self-worth. A.J. Swoboda said it this way: "For the addict, the biggest struggle isn't loving others. Addicts can be very compassionate and kind toward others. Mostly, addicts struggle to love themselves, because addicts have let themselves down so many times." [24] Addicts tend to feel that they don't deserve to be loved.

Remember, the evil one, who hates you and hates God's love, will pull back on his bowstring and shoot flaming arrows of shame and disbelief at your mind, trying to convince you, like He tried to convince Jesus in the wilderness, that you're not God's beloved child.

---

[23] Les Parrott, Ph.D. & Neil Clark , Ph.D , *Love the Life You Live.* , (Tyndale House Publishers,2004), 67.

[24] A.J. Swoboda, *A Glorious Dark*, (Baker Books, 2014), 62.

Every thought of rejection will be responded to with a declaration of how much God loves me.

Every thought of hopelessness will be met with a positive statement about my present thankfulness.

I'm learning to live by grace, and base my worth on God's love for me, not on my production or performance.

When the death-dealer shoots arrows at your mind, shoot back, just like Jesus did. Have your quiver filled with scriptures and statements that retort and extinguish his lies with truth like Christ did when He said to Satan: "It is written …" Talk back to your thoughts. Even if you feel unworthy of His love, keep speaking His word, which promises that His love will not fail.

God loves you even if you feel unworthy, but He loves you too much to leave you feeling that way.

God loves you *even if* your *even if's* sound terrible. Let me introduce you to a God who is, in the words of A.J. Swoboda, inebriated with *agape* love: "The gospel is a piece of terribly delightful news that you and I and everyone in history have craved so desperately to hear. The gospel is that God is drunk with love, and He won't get sober." [25]

---

[25] Ibid, 54.

Chapter Nine – A Wing and A Prayer

My friend Rick is a world-class hang-glider. His longest flight was 197 miles. His highest flight was 18,000 feet. It amazes me that he is still alive.

Death knocked on his door several years ago when he was flying over the southeastern Oregon desert. He saw a dust devil that indicated the presence of a strong thermal. When he saw the dust, he was flying at 10,500 feet and decided to fly into the thermal and let it lift him to his target altitude of 13,500.

The thermal didn't lift him gently though. It shook him violently until one of his glider's wings collapsed. As Rick began a vicious spiral, he struggled to reach his ripcord. He finally did, and with prayer, one wing, and a partially opened parachute, he slammed into a tall fir tree, breaking limbs one after another until his parachute caught in a tree and he came to a halt less than a yard from terra-firma. [26] Rick literally came down, in the words of a famous World War II song, with "A Wing and a Prayer."

---

[26] Ken Johnson, *Life² – The Secret to Limitless Living* (Foursquare Media, 2007), 9.

In the last chapter I talked about God's *even if* love. What would your main *even if* be? Maybe you need to realize that God loves you *even if* your father didn't. Or perhaps you need to trust God who loves you *even if* you turned your back on him and walked away. When I was in high school, I saw a friend name Mike look up to heaven and say with bitterness, "I damn you God." Mike needed God to love him, *even if* he hated God. (A few years ago, some fifty years after Mike's blasphemous curse, He came into a living relationship with the forgiving, loving God that he once cursed.)

As I headed back to work after my emergency summer sabbatical, I leaned on God, being aware that He loved me passionately even if I was damaged, like a bird with a broken wing. I sensed His love surrounding me, coming to me directly, via staff members who cared about me.

More relational

I decided to eat lunch with the staff every work-day. I'd been ignoring lunch for several years, but I had changed. I slowed down and took the time to build deeper relationships with my co-workers. Several staff members came to me privately and said how they much they appreciated me being more available and relational.

People became more important to me than projects. I saw people through new eyes. Because I had changed, my relationships changed. There was new life in my relationship with God and with other people.

Our relationships have a vertical and horizontal axis. As I became convinced of my worth in God's heart and eyes, that strengthening of my vertical relationship axis also strengthened and improved my horizontal relationship axis – my relationships with people.

First, I learned how to believe, receive and rest in God's love. I'm going to be celebrating that love forever. The more I learn of Him and His amazing love, the more I'll think about it, talk about it, sing about it and soak in it.

Second, my horizontal relationship axis grew stronger. I have a new compassion for people who are emotionally wounded. Before I experienced deep depression, my attitude toward depressed people tended to be, *"Get over it. Get up and get going."* But a trip to the dark valley, where you wonder if you'll ever make it through the valley, changes you.

My relationships have changed in a basic way because I am no longer worried about proving my worth to friends, old or new.

In their helpful book, *Love the Life You Live*, Les Parrott and Neal Warren describe what happens when a person comes to believe he or she matters to God: "Your needs of significance are already met; you are free to simply enjoy authentic interactions for their own sake." [27] Knowing I was radically loved by God caused me to experience a new level of aliveness socially, mentally and spiritually.

[27] Les Parrott, Ph.D. & Neil Clark Warren, Ph.D. *Love the Life You Live* (Tyndale House Publishers, 2004), 79.

No one other than me can block me from being a person who is becoming increasingly alive with every passing moment, even as I approach the day when I die physically and graduate into a whole new dimension of aliveness.

The murderous evil one tried to destroy me, but God turned the table on him and created a 'more relational, more relaxed me.' I am amazed by the way God brings good out of bad. God is incredibly efficient, bringing life out of death and joy out of sorrow. His agape love trumps the plots of the evil one, who hates God and hates love.

God IS love

"God loves you." I put these words on a large stone at the main exit of Westside Church. What better phrase to take home with you after church?

The Bible says that in the last days "the love of many will grow cold. [28] I see that happening all around me. People are love-starved. They don't get love and they don't give love. We have frostbitten souls.

The gospel, the good news of God's love, is the only thing that can warm those souls. Brennan Manning called Jesus' attraction to the unattractive "the mystery of the Gospel."

---

[28] Tyndale House Publishers. (2013). *Holy Bible: New Living Translation* (Mt 24:12). Carol Stream, IL: Tyndale House Publishers

Little wonder that John 3:16 is the most popular verse in the Bible. It says that God loves the world. The world in that verse is not the planet, or the humanistic world system, but people, the eight billion individuals on the planet today. Read about the way Christ treated people and you'll see that God loves the world, one person at a time. God is great at loving. He is so good at loving because what He does (love) is what He is (love). He is the verb love and the noun love.

I believe that love existed before people did. God the Father, God the Son, and God the Spirit loved one another before God created the universe and the world. *Love* is one being expressing compassion and affection for another. The triune Godhead possessed and experienced love before God created mankind.

Because God is love, He could create love. People exist because of love, and they exist to be loved. God has more than eight billion kids, and He loves them all, one at a time. He loves each one as if he or she were the only one. In sports terms, everyone is on His first string.

Remember that story I told about getting put back on the eighth grade B-Team just before the biggest game of the season? That wounded me deeply. I didn't realize the wound hadn't healed until I was benched by depression 42 years later. I still struggled with self-worth, feeling like a 'scrub.'

At one point early in my season of depression I was on a road trip when, without warning, the depression dump-truck unloaded a ton of sadness on me. I sank lower and lower under the crushing load until tears began to run down my cheeks.

I pulled the car over and whispered to God, "I feel like I did in the eighth grade. I feel like a loser. I feel like I'm back on the B-Team." I didn't hear it out loud, but I did hear it clearer than I had ever heard God's voice: "I don't even have a B-Team. Everyone, including you, is on my A Team."

Seeing myself through the eyes of God was like breaking out of prison for me. I grew to recognize and totally believe in my value now and forever.

God is love. God is kind. God thinks everybody is important, valuable, and special. Everyone. That includes me. That includes you. People were drawn to Jesus Christ, not because of how He looked *to them*, but because of how He looked *at them*.

Love is the very center of who God is. He loves us because of Who He is, not because of who we are. He doesn't love us 'if.' He loves us *even if*.

When I read what A.J. Swoboda, one of my favorite authors, said about God's *agape* love I almost jumped out of my chair and started dancing: "To be precise, this is a unique kind of love few of us could imagine. To put it in the simplest of terms, God's love is the only kind of love – in contrast to all other kinds of love we might seek in our world – that is renewable, organic, sustainable, and local. God's love is a free-range, cage-free kind of love, gushing wildly through every nook and cranny of God's wild creation. God's love is an ocean with no shores. God loves us that way, the way the Father loves Jesus." [29]

When I came back home and received unconditional love from my wife, kids, grandkids, close friends, and my church, I realized that their love for me was not based on my success or failure. Their love for me was an echo of God's totally unconditional love.

A month or so after I got back to Westside Church, I carefully shared with my church family what I had gone through. The outpouring of love was amazing. I received a mountain of cards and letters. Many people confided in me and said they were going or had gone through something similar. The shortest distance between two people, heart to heart, is a story. Person after person said, "You should share your story in a book."

You are reading the results. In my wildest dreams, I couldn't imagine that the path to my rescue and restoration would be the path that led to a radical new awareness of my being loved. Like the Bible says, "God's ways are not man's ways." (Isaiah 55:8) How true!

Thanks to God's grace and an amazing staff, Westside Church continued to grow during the time I was gone and when I came back partially recovered.

Believe it

---

[29] A.J. Swoboda, *A Glorious Dark*, 89.

Seeing yourself as valuable, or having others see you as such, is not about achieving, it's about believing and receiving. It's about believing God's love is big enough to embrace you right where you are and just as you are.

You might say, "Prove that." I can't. But God can.

God knows it's hard for us to believe He really does love us, so He proved it: "This is how God showed his love for us: God sent his only Son into the world, so we might live through him. This is the kind of love we are talking about—not that we once upon a time loved God, but that he loved us and sent his Son as a sacrifice to clear away our sins and the damage they've done to our relationship with God." [30] God didn't just talk about His love, He proved it, through the way Jesus lived and died.

Do you believe that verse you just read? Maybe your answer to that question would be the same as the answer that the father of a sick son gave Jesus when Jesus asked him if he believed He could heal the boy: "I do believe. Help me overcome my unbelief." (Luke 2:9) Go ahead. Say it to God. Write it on a piece of paper and put it in your pocket. Jesus didn't chastise the weak-faith-father, He just healed his son.

And when He answers your prayer and helps you overcome your unbelief, your faith will receive His love.

You will find the truth of what the Spirit of God said through the Apostle Paul: "No power in the sky above or in the earth

---

[30] Peterson, E. H. (2005). *The Message: the Bible in contemporary language* (1 Jn 4:9-10). Colorado Springs, CO: NavPress.

below—indeed, nothing in all creation will ever be able to separate us from the love of God that is revealed in Christ Jesus our Lord." [31]

God is an ocean of *agape*, a universe of *agape*. Go to the highest place, His love is there. Go to the lowest place, His love is there. Where East meets West and where North meets South, His love is there. He is head over heels in love with you. Your picture is on His refrigerator. I'm not just trying to be cute. His love is serious business. It killed His Son. It saved my life.

Don't just visit His love, dwell there. Here's His invitation to you. These words came from His heart, "Live in my love." [32] Get off the shore of doubt and dive into God's love. As Mr. Swoboda says, "Faith is drowning in a torrent of God's love. [33]

Second Touch

My down times in the past five plus years have been mild compared to my original depression because my identity is not based on my work, or my accomplishments, but on God's love.

After being diagnosed with Parkinson's, I didn't want to be an ostrich, sticking my head in the sand, so, as I mentioned

---

[31] Tyndale House Publishers. (2013). *Holy Bible: New Living Translation* (Ro 8:39). Carol Stream, IL: Tyndale House Publishers.

[32] GOD'S WORD Translation, John 15:9

[33] A. J. Swoboda, *A Glorious Dark*, 89.

earlier, Linda and I began to research the disease and its ramifications.

I believe God still heals people, and I'm continuing to follow what Jesus taught about persistent prayer.

I'm also thankful for Sinemet and other meds that have been discovered in the last couple of decades. It usually masks some of the physical symptoms of PD for five years or so. To date, I've been able to continue to take my bird dogs hunting, but walking on uneven, rocky ground is a challenge. I predetermined that I will be thankful for *what I have left* and not focused on *what I have lost*.

A while back I decided, with my doctor's consent, to phase out my depression meds. I did pretty well for a week or two, then I began to feel a bit blue. I caught myself thinking like I did when I was in my nosedive. I prayed and fought against those thoughts, and my depression was not even half as deep as it once had been, but life seemed a little bit cold and dark.

Then I got down on myself for being depressed and began to feel even more depressed. *Hadn't I become victorious over this whole thing? Why was I asking God for help with depression again?* I felt that due to lack of faith, I had partially lost my soul's healing.

Then my thinking went to the Bible story about a man Jesus healed in two stages. In stage one, the guy got to see light and blurry blobs. It was a new thing for him, and he was totally excited, but he sensed there was more. He told Jesus, "I see men as trees walking." Jesus touched his eyes again and he saw things clearly with 20/20 vision. God showed me that I needed a second touch too.

> Sometimes we don't fully see what God wants us to see, even after He has given us more insight than we've ever had before. We need a second touch.

> ⊡Touched by Jesus, the blind man said, "I see people; they look like trees walking around." Once more Jesus put his hands on the man's eyes. Then his eyes were opened, his sight was restored, and he saw everything clearly. (Mark 8:24-25, NIV)

> God has recently touched my eyes the second time, helping me see even better that I can live a life based on His love.

Maybe you believe in God's love. You can see it but it's a still a little blurry. Press in the way the blind man did. Ask for a second touch.

If you decide to believe and receive God's love, don't be discouraged by temporary down times. Just keep building your house, your whole life, on the firm foundation of His love. Keep filling your heart and mind with the truth of His love for you.

In the first part of Mark 8, the story is told of Jesus making a meal into a feast for thousands, a second time. After two similar miracles, the disciples didn't see what they should have seen. Their lack of faith upset Jesus, but He refused to give up on them. He patiently continued to teach them and graciously gave them a third, fourth and fifth touch.

I knew I needed another touch from God because I sensed that He was probing even deeper than He did in my dark night. New challenges and new experiences caused fear and anxiety to come to the surface. Once again, as in my earlier season of depression, I decided to believe God. Where the evil one intends to make me less alive, God will, through grace and faith, make me more alive by showing me how to live a steady, balanced life.

Re-fired

I began to sense that my time as Lead Pastor of Westside Church was drawing to a close. I had been preparing a young man on our pastoral staff to take my position. I had known and admired this young man, Steve, since he was in the fifth grade. Over a three year span I began giving Steve more and more responsibility until finally handing off the baton. I remained on staff part time for two more years.

The transition went so smoothly that our denominational leaders called it "amazing." Loss of a long-term senior pastor in a large church usually results in a 10-20 percent decrease in attendance and giving. Westside didn't miss a beat. It kept going and growing, as it is to this day.

One thing that helped me stay out of the way during and after the Westside transition was that, after what I'd learned from my near-death dive of depression, I didn't have my self-worth tied in with being a lead pastor.

> *I find myself making my first footprints in the scary land of 'semi-retirement.' I'm speaking, writing and coaching, but I actually have a little bit of free time. It's a whole new experience. I'm at the border of a new era, like the Israelites on the edge of the Promised Land.*
>
> *God told His people to listen carefully and obey completely so they would "... know which way to go, since you have never been this way before."*

I'll never really retire. I'll re-purpose and re-enlist and re-fire! For me, retirement is experiencing God's purposes in a new dimension.

> *Retirement is not stopping. It is experiencing God's purposes in a new dimension. Thirty-six months after stepping back and stepping down as Lead Pastor, I am thriving and thankful.*

Looking back, I am amazed by God's ability to bring good from bad. When I review my emotional plummet, I thank God that He let it happen. I'm happier, more solid, more at ease, and more blessed than ever. I know God used my crisis as my crucible. Change is always preceded by challenge.

Looking forward, I see that when God brings me to a difficult boundary requiring trust in Him, I have to decide whether I will fearfully hold on to the 'old me' or let go of who I was and courageously embrace who I am in Christ. I've never been who I am about to become.

One of the things I remember about my days of deep depression was that I couldn't seem to look forward. By this I mean I couldn't think of one thing I actually anticipated with excitement and pleasure. I didn't look forward to anything, and I didn't feel like I would ever be able to look forward to anything again. Now, I wake up every morning looking forward to a great day. I feel like I have a thousand things to look forward to. I'm very thankful.

More and more, I'm looking forward to the next era, the next chapter of my life story. God has always given me revelation about my life in seven-year eras. When I semi-retired five years ago, God spoke to me about my next seven-year era, and I wrote this in my journal:

> I know God is not done changing, improving, upgrading me. I know He is more interested in what He can do in me than in what He can do for me.
>
> I want to finish this season well, and enthusiastically dive into my next seven-year assignment.

I began to sense a positive direction from God for my next seven years.

I believe God is calling me to teach and write in my next season. I am excited about that, filled with happy anticipation.

I felt today that the Spirit may have said, "Start the writing with 'It All Comes Down to This.'"

I've grown to the point where I know that my God-given life message is, "God loves you and invites you into His amazing aliveness."

I firmly believe that I am going higher into eternal aliveness with every day of my life. I believe the next era will be my most eternally fruitful seven-year period to date.

I believe that the last day of my presence on this planet will be the most alive day I will have lived. No one other than myself can block me from being a person who is becoming increasingly alive with every passing moment.

That doesn't sound like a journal entry by a depressed person, does it? No, it's a journal entry of a recovered person who keeps recovering and wants to help others recover. I'm a child of the Living God – that is my core identity, the source of my dignity and healthy self-regard.

I'm going to be celebrating God's great love forever. The more I learn of Him and His amazing love, the more I will embrace it.

Given God's help, I can honestly continue to close my emails with a proclamation that rings true from the core of my being ... "Better and Better."

Love is the reason I am better than ever. I'm learning to find my identity in His love.

I have so much more to learn about God's love! I'll start with what I share next.

Chapter Ten – Near Life

My high-school friend Janice and some of her friends were at a favorite swimming hole where a cliff could be climbed to the top of a waterfall. She had nearly reached the top when she slipped and fell backward, flailing her arms in the air and screaming.

She landed on her back in hard dirt with a sickening thud. The impact would have cracked her skull, except she had a swimming cap on her head, and had a towel folded and tucked behind her head under the cap. The cap and towel may have saved her life.

Years later, Janice told me about a strange thing that happened when she fell. She said that in the few seconds before she hit the ground, everything went into super slow motion in her mind. She saw several reruns of incidents from her past, and then several previews of her future.

What she saw about her future must have been prophetic because some of the things she pictured as she fell came to pass in the time between when she fell and when we talked a few years later. I've never heard of another near-death experience like the one Janice described.

She said, "I can't begin to explain how I could see those pictures, flash-backs and previews in not much more than a split-second. Several hours of thoughts about my past and my future were crammed into those two amazing seconds."

She went on to say that she has never struggled with the preciousness of her life or the meaning of her life since that day. She knows she is alive for a reason. Those pictures started her on a quest of progressive discovery, including discovering more about God and about herself.

Janice's near-death situation left her nearer to real, full life. Likewise, I believe a person can come out of a near-death emotional nosedive and actually be more alive than before their crisis. I did, and I am. I am happier, more secure, more at ease, more blessed, and more alive than ever.

Accepting God's acceptance of me, I have found bedrock for an abundant life. Love is the reason I am better than ever. I'm learning to find my identity in His love. In my quiet time this morning, I sang to God the astounding but simple words from the worship song *Good Good Father*: "I'm loved by you, it's who I am." [34]

Live in love

John, one of the twelve original apostles of Jesus Christ, said it this way: "We know how much God loves us, and we have

[34] Written by Anthony Brown and Pat Barrett (worship band Housefires) and sung also by Chris Tomlin.

[35] Tyndale House Publishers. (2013). *Holy Bible: New Living Translation* (1 Jn 4:16). Carol Stream, IL: Tyndale House Publishers.

put our trust in his love. God is love, and all who live in love live in God, and God lives in them." [35] If you really believe in God's love, you can, as John said, "live in His love."

God loved me before I went into my emotional nosedive, and He would have loved me even if I crashed. But I didn't crash, and I won't. I won't because I am convinced that He loves me, and that He loves me with a love so solid that I can base my worth and my life on it. That conviction saved my life.

I am accepted in the beloved, in Christ. When I pray, I don't come to God in my name, I come in Jesus' Name.

Last month I bought Linda a gold necklace with a small gold plate on it. The jeweler agreed to engrave a word of my choice on the necklace. I chose the word 'Loved.' I wanted Linda to remember that she is loved, and always will be loved.

If I wore a necklace it would have a cross on it and would be engraved with two priceless words from John 3:16: "So Loved." I'd wear it like a price tag. The cross speaks of the value God places on me. Christ loves me. He laid down His life so that I could receive abundant, eternal life. I know I am loved, but I am loved more than I will ever know. As I wrote in my journal during my personal daybreak:

> *God loves me ferociously and unconditionally.*
> *As this amazing awareness grows on me,*
> *calluses are coming off of my heart and*
> *cataracts are coming off of my eyes.*

As I came out of the tunnel of depression, I set my mind to savor every day of my life, and to try to improve a little bit each day. I figured that if I could improve one percent a week, I would double in ability after 70 weeks. I have a list of ten practical areas where I'm reading, learning, applying and improving.

When I complete one of my ten challenges, I add another improvement goal to keep the number at ten. I plan to be a life-long learner. I hope to still be working on improving on the day I draw my last breath.

My self-development goals are challenging, but attainable. They deal with improving at hobbies, staying in shape, improving at writing, speaking, listening and learning.

For instance, I plan to hike the Grand Canyon again.

Last year, I hiked six miles into the canyon and six miles out in a day. Parkinson's Disease made it twice as hard for me; my last thousand steps required a thousand individual decisions to keep going. Next year, I plan to hike all the way to the Colorado River and out in one day. Fifteen miles of challenging travel on challenging terrain with Parkinson's attacking my balance and coordination. I have Parkinson's but it doesn't have me!

I'm riding a bike while I still can. I'm running three or four times a week, even as PD makes it hard to not trip and fall. I'm doing yoga to help maintain my balance. I'm being careful about my eating, and I'm playing brain games on my computer to keep my mind as sharp as possible.

The point is, I've set some challenging but reachable goals for personal development. If I expect to make massive gains in short time periods, I'd probably get discouraged and give up. But if I take one day at a time, I can gain one percent a day, and that compounds rapidly.

Emotional fitness is interwoven with physical fitness. I'm working just as hard on staying fit emotionally and psychologically as I am physically.

I read challenging books. I write. I participate in classes and seminars that help me improve my speaking and writing. I spend time reading the Bible and praying. Mental calisthenics.

I do my best to stay fit spiritually, mentally, physically and emotionally. My deepest awareness of myself is that I am deeply loved by Jesus Christ. My life is no longer about proving my worth to others through what I do.

Every day I'm learning more about God's extravagant love. It's like I'm getting my master's degree at Agape University, majoring in 'God loves me.'

I remember biology classes in High School. The first part of the class was the teacher talking with us, and the final part of the class took place in the lab so we could have hands-on experience related to what we had just learned in the lecture.

Similarly, I look at my life as a lecture/lab experience. As I read the Bible, and read good books, I am being taught. Then

I go to the lab, for hands-on work, where I see for myself what the lecture proposed to be true.

Think-Right

We have three department stores in town with similar names that confuse me: Rite Aid; Best Buy and Bi-Mart. I tend to call them all 'Buy-Rite.' (Linda keeps saying, "There is no Buy-Rite.") If I opened a counseling center that doubled as a store that sold peace and success and joy, I'd call the store 'Think Right.'

As I said earlier, I'm learning more about thinking correctly. I'm learning how to stay off elephant trails of pessimism and depression. What I learned in the Bible and at The Center is being reinforced by what I learn about PD from recent research.

What I learned at The Center about making new, positive mental paths has been confirmed by the things I've since learned. Medical doctors and scientists are talking a lot about neuroplasticity – brain changeability - these days. Scholars have discovered that repeated mental experience actually changed the neurons in the brain.

With Parkinson's Disease, neurons in the brain build up excess proteins that form plaque that blocks the signals between brain neurons. Researchers have learned that the brain has an amazing ability to re-educate undamaged neurons and thus find new thought pathways. In the intriguing book "The Brain's Way of Healing," Norman

Doidge speaks about the way the brain's synaptic connections are established and strengthened.

"As a child learns the alphabet, the visual shape of the letter A is connected with the sound "ay." Each time the child looks at the letter and repeats the sound, the neurons involved "fire together" at the same time, and then "wire together": The synaptic connections between them are strengthened." [36]

As I mentioned earlier in the book, as we choose to think and speak positive thoughts, new synaptic pathways are created in the brain. Researchers can actually watch this happen on brain scans. Doidge says, "When we think particular thoughts, certain networks in the brain are "turned on," while others are switched off... Once a relevant circuit is turned on by a thought, it fires, and the blood flows to that circuit ... to replenish its energy supply." [37]

Neurons actually compete for limited mental real estate, because "the activities the brain performs regularly take up more and more space in the brain by "stealing" resources from other areas." [38]

Get this. You and I, as an act of our will, can choose to think positive thoughts, and by doing so, change the organ inside our skulls.

---

[36] Norman Doidge, MD , *The Brain's Way of Healing*, (Penguin Books, 2015), 9.

[37] Ibid., Doidge, 109-110

[38] Ibid, 11

People helpers

People who go through severe depression and don't crash are poised to help others who are discouraged, burned out and depressed. One of the people who read this book and gave me feedback sent this email to me: "The subject is so important and yet still something people tend to hide away – the book made me feel like you would be an honest and effective mentor for people as they walk toward solutions."

Looking back, I see that God is very good at bringing good things out of bad things. I know God used my crisis as His crucible. Change is always preceded by challenge. And I know God is not done changing, improving and upgrading me. I know He is more interested in what He can *do in me and through me, than what He can do in me* and *for me.*

Emerging slowly from the darkest of dark places, I stepped into the sunlight of bright new aliveness. As the Psalmist said, "You have made known to me the path of life; you will fill me with joy in your presence, with eternal pleasures at your right hand." (Psalm 16:11)

The evil one, the one Jesus called "the thief," came to "steal and kill and destroy." [39] He targets Larry, Stan, Rick, Frank, you and me. I'm happy to know he will fail with all five of us. And we are all more willing and able to help people who are experiencing what we experienced.

---

[39] Tyndale House Publishers. (2013). *Holy Bible: New Living Translation* (Jn 10:10). Carol Stream, IL: Tyndale House Publishers

You Matter

You were created to be loved. The first question is not "How much do you love God?" The first questions is "How much does God love you?"

God loves you so much that He sacrificed His Son in order that you and He could be reconnected forever. God does not love you because you are good, He loves you because He is good, and He is love.

God's love is passionate and aggressive. The powerful worship song 'Reckless Love' describes it this way: "Oh, the overwhelming, never-ending, reckless love of God ... I couldn't earn it, and I don't deserve it, still you give Yourself away ... " [40]

God's love is the main reason we were created ... the distilled essence of the entire Bible ... it's the thing that outlasts everything else.

God's love is sure. God's love is a given; it is given to you "in Christ." It is an amazing thing to be warmly accepted by God in Christ. The amazement doubles when you accept your acceptance. In the name of God's love, just as my counselors and my friends challenged me, I challenge you.

My challenge to you

---

[40] Reckless Love, Cory Asbury / Caleb Culver / Ran Jackson. Lyrics © Bethel Music Publishing Sony/ATV Music Publishing LLC

First, **I challenge you to open yourself to God's love.** Don't reject God's love. Don't mistrust His devotion. I challenge you to choose to believe Him when He says He loves you. God loves you just as you are, not as you ought to be, because you'll never in this lifetime be all that you ought to be. If your heart is open, agape love will find its way in.

Second, **I challenge you to spend time alone with God.** As Brennan Manning said, "We must have time alone with God if we are to be aware of our belovedness." [41]

I gladly echo the challenge of Les Parrott PhD and Neil Clark, PhD to let God's love seep down in your soul "... until you know at the center of your being that your value is established for all time. You don't have to work harder or look better. Significance is not about achieving, it's about receiving." [42]

Third, **I challenge you to read the Bible and meditate on its message of love.** Marinate in scripture. Study what the scriptures say about who you are. Read the book of John. There you will see that Jesus is God's way of saying, "I love you." John's gospel is full of good news about God's offer of deeper, richer living. John called himself "The disciple Jesus loved." I hope you come to think of yourself that way too.

Next, **I challenge you to find a community of 'loved people,' people who know that God loves them.**

---

[41] Brennan Manning, *Abba's Child*, pg. 53

[42] Les Parrott, Ph.D. & Neil Clark, Ph.D. (Tyndale House Publishers, 2004), 57.

I'm so thankful to be part of a community of Christians who know they are not perfect and know they are still loved. Our leaders work hard to live out scriptures like this: "Regarding life together and getting along with each other, you don't need me to tell you what to do. You're God-taught in these matters. Just love one another! [43]

The theme of our church is 'Life / Love / Jesus.' Our church family truly does love God and love people. That's because we know we are loved, and loved people love people. "Inside your Temple, O God, we think of your constant love." [44]

You may think that there is not a church like that in your area, but there is. Get serious. Look hard. You'll find it, and you will fill up your love tank every time you meet together. Remember, there is no such thing as a perfect church, because there are no perfect people.

Fourth, **I challenge you to get help**. If you have a family member or friend that is in an emotional nosedive or headed for one, find help in your church family or your community.

Get help from close friends. Get counsel from gifted counselors.

If your friend who needs help is a people helper, remember that people who have a vocation or calling that entails

---

[43] Peterson, E. H. (2005). *The Message: the Bible in contemporary language* (1 Th 4:9). Colorado Springs, CO: NavPress.

[44] American Bible Society. (1992). The Holy Bible: The Good news Translation (2nd ed., Ps 48:9). New York: American Bible Society.

helping other people are often the last to realize that they need help.

In stubborn pride, I almost waited too long. I believe that if I hadn't humbled myself and sought Christian counsel, I would be deeply impaired today.

You can recover from your emotional quandary. You can recover from your spiritual nosedive. I know, because I have. I've made a huge recovery, and I'm still in process.

I challenge you to accept your acceptance. Don't come to God in your own name, counting on your own performance, but come boldly in Jesus' Name.

Discover what it means to live by grace. Do what I did when Brennan Manning spoke to me through his book Abba's Child: "Accept God's love for you. Define yourself by it. Live by it." [45]

Believing and receiving God's great love was the primary key to my recovery. I was burned out and hopeless. The evil one was whispering to me, "You'll never recover from this." But I did. I found my legs in God's love.

Next, **I challenge you to keep going.** I remember what it feels like to try to navigate the day when all is darkness, and there isn't even a hint of hope.

I kept saying, "I WILL NOT give up, and I WILL NOT give in." ~~Don't bow out. Don't become~~ a hermit. Don't even consider

[45] Brennan. Manning – *Abba's Child.* Pg. 51

suicide. I'm here to say, "I made it through my pitch-black darkness, and you can too."

Don't be discouraged by temporary down times. Just keep building you house, your whole life, on the firm foundation of God's love.

Finally, I challenge you to let the love of God, the love that saturates your life, spill over on others. Living in an awareness of God's love - vertical vitality – causes a person to care for and build up others – horizontal vitality.

Jesus, the greatest Lover of all times, knew He was loved by His Papa in Heaven. Before He entered His three years of life-giving ministry, before He entered a lonely, barren wilderness, Jesus, standing in the Jordan River, heard His Father say that He loved His Son.

The Father didn't say this after Jesus proclaimed the good news, healed the sick, taught the disciples and died on the cross. He spoke His love before Jesus kicked off His formal ministry. The Father didn't love Him after what He did or because of what He did, but before He did what He did.

Jesus, who forgave those who murdered Him while they were in the ugly act, loved like no one else has ever loved. He loved because He was loved. You see, loved people love people. When we quit working, sweating and striving to earn God's love, we have new energy to love others, including the unlovely.

Love Wins

God is very good at bringing good things out of bad things. When I look back on my emotional plummet, I thank God He let it happen. I'm happier, more solid, more at ease, more blessed than ever. My emotional death spiral was not terminal.

I'm going to be celebrating God's great love forever. The more I learn of Him and His amazing love, the more I'll think about it, talk about it, sing about it, soak in it, and live in it.

I believe that love, the God kind of love, is stronger than anything else, and that it outlasts everything else.

If you're fortunate enough to honestly to answer the question "Do you matter?" with a "Yes," the next question might be "Why do you matter?" The answer permanently attached to my heart five years ago is still my answer today. "I matter because I matter to God. I matter because God values me and loves me, and nothing can separate me from His love."

A man who imprisoned and executed Christians, a man named Paul, miraculously came to accept God's forgiveness and love, then wrote these words about the God kind of love: "Can anything ever separate us from Christ's love? Does it mean he no longer loves us if we have trouble or calamity, or are persecuted, or hungry, or destitute, or in danger, or threatened with death? ... No, despite all these things, overwhelming victory is ours through Christ, who loved us." (Romans 8:35, 37)

My Prayer for You

I wrote this book to help you, and those you care for and I believe God knew I would write it and you would read it. I pray that it has opened your eyes to the largeness of God's love.

In the Ephesus church of the first century, people were going through some hard times. Some of them must have been wondering if God really loved them. Prompted by God's Spirit, Paul, the man I mentioned above, the man devoted to sharing God's love, wrote this message to them: "And I ask him that with both feet planted firmly on love, you'll be able to take in with all followers of Jesus the extravagant dimensions of Christ's love. Reach out and experience the breadth! Test its length! Plumb the depths! Rise to the heights! Live full lives, full in the fullness of God." [46]

And I add this prayer to that. Please pray this prayer. If you can find a private place where you can pray out loud, do it.

Loving Father, thank you for helping me be aware of my emotional nosedive. I'm going to pull out of this thing because I do believe you love me, warts and all. I want to believe it even more, so I ask you, like that man in the

---

[46] Peterson, E. H. (2005). *The Message: the Bible in contemporary language* (Eph 3:17–19). Colorado Springs, CO: NavPress.

Bible did, "Help me believe." Please keep convincing me that I matter to you.

I understand that faith is not just a feeling, it is a choice and an action. I choose to believe in your love for me even in the times when I don't feel loved.

I ask for your grace, for your unmerited love and favor. I can't earn it. I receive it as a gift from you.

Dear God, teach me how to live in your love. Make the Bible come alive to me so I can come alive to you. I don't want to live a shallow life. I want to live in your boundless love.

Help me, as I understand and believe your love at a deeper level, to invest more of my time in loving others as you have always loved me.

Help my friends who are stuck; help them break free.

Thank you for being Love-In-Action, dear God.

Made in the USA
San Bernardino, CA
11 November 2019